بسم الله الرحمن الرحيم

I LOVE ISLAM

1

CD Included

ISLAMIC STUDIES TEXTBOOK SERIES - LEVEL ONE

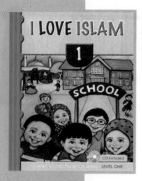

I Love Islam 1

بسم الله الرحمن الرحيم

In the Name of Allah, Most Compassionate, Most Merciful

I Love Islam© is a series of Islamic Studies text-books that gradually introduces Muslim students to the essentials of their faith. It brings to light the historic and cultural aspects of Islam. The series covers levels one through five, which are suitable for young learners. It includes student textbooks and workbooks, as well as teacher and parent guides.

The Islamic Services Foundation is undertaking this project in collaboration with Brighter Horizons Academy in Dallas, Texas. Extensive efforts have been made to review the enclosed material. However, constructive suggestions and comments that would enrich the content of this work are welcome.

All praise is due to Allah (God) for providing us with the resources that have enabled us to complete the first part of this series. This is an ongoing project, and it is our sincere wish and hope that it will impact our Muslim children today and for many years to come.

Copyright © 2018 by Islamic Services Foundation

ISBN 1-933301-20-4

All rights reserved. No part of this publication may be reproduced or transmitted in any form or by any means, electronic or mechanical, including photocopy, recording, or any information storage and retrieval system, without permission in writing from the publisher.

PROGRAM DIRECTOR *
Nabil Sadoun, Ed.D.

WRITING TEAM
Aimen Ansari
Nabil Sadoun, Ed.D.
Majida Yousef

REVIEWERS AND ADVISORS
Susan Douglass
Freda Shamma, Ph.D.

CONTRIBUTORS
Isam Alimam
Ummukulthum Al-Maawiy
Lana Baghal Dasti
Suzy Fouad
Nicholas Howard
Bushra Zawi
Menat Zihni

CURRICULUM DESIGN
Majida Salem
Nabil Sadoun, Ed.D.

ENGLISH EDITOR
Sumaiya Susan Gavell

GRAPHIC DESIGN
Mohammed Asad

ILLUSTRATIONS
Sujata Bansal
Ramendranath Sarkar
Special thanks to:
Goodword Books

ISLAMIC SONGS AND POEMS
Noor Saadeh
NoorArt, Inc.

PHOTOGRAPHY
Al-Anwar Designs
Isam Alimam

PUBLISHER AND OWNER

ISF PUBLICATIONS

Islamic Services Foundation
P.O. Box 451623
Garland, Texas 75045
U.S.A
Tel: +1 972-414-5090
Fax: +1 972-414-5640
www.myislamicbooks.com

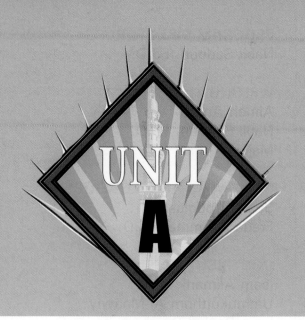

UNIT A

MY BELOVED ALLAH

UNIT B

MY GREAT PROPHET

UNIT C

WORSHIPPING ALLAH

UNIT D

MY MUSLIM WORLD

MY MUSLIM MANNERS

I Love Islam Friends and Family

Zaid

Leena

Mr. Mahmood

Mrs. Mahmood

Bilal

Sarah

Mr. Siraj

Mrs. Siraj

Amir

Omar

Mona

Khalid

Ahmad

Teacher Hibah

Baby Yousuf

UNIT **A**

MY BELOVED ALLAH

Allah, Our Great Creator

questions?

1. Have you ever seen a star shining in the night sky?
2. What has Allah created?
3. Who makes eyeglasses and cameras?
4. Who made your eyes?
5. Who made the Earth as a home for all living things?

word watch

Allah	اللّه
Subhan'Allah	سُبْحانَ اللّه
masjid	مَسْجِدْ
masajid	مَساجِدْ
Al-Khaliq	الخَالِقْ
Al-Musawwir	المُصَوّرْ
Al-Bari'	البَارِيء
du'aa'	دُعاءْ

A toy maker made this beautiful toy.

A builder made this nice house.

Who made the world?

When we look at the Earth, the sky, mountains, animals, and people, we know that they were all created by **Allah**, the only Creator.

"Allah" is the Arabic word for God.
It means: *The one God we worship.*

healthy
habit

Say "*Subhan'Allah*"

سُبْحـانَ اللّه

when you see something beautiful or great. This means "Glory be to Allah."

Allah (is) Al-Khaliq

الـخالِقَ

THE CREATOR

He created the **Earth** for us to live on.

He created the **sun** to give us light and warmth during the day.

He also made the **moon** to give us light during the night.

Allah **is** Al-Bari'

البارِيء

THE MAKER

Allah created the whole world. He created billions and billions of stars and planets. He alone made every living and nonliving thing.

سُبْحَانَ اللّه

Subhan'Allah!

ALLAH GAVE US EVERYTHING WE NEED TO LIVE.

Allah gave us the **soil** to grow **food.**

He gave us **homes** to live in.

He gave us **friends** and **family** so that we do not feel lonely.

"وجعلنا من الماء كل شيء حي"

"...and made from water every living thing."
Al Anbia 30

WE ALL NEED WATER TO LIVE. ALLAH GAVE US WATER TO DRINK AND TO CLEAN OUR-SELVES.

WATER:
The most perfect drink for all living things.

Allah also helps us make many useful things.

- houses
- cars
- schools
- *masajid* (more than one *masjid*)
- clothes
- food

He gave us intelligence to use when making good things.

Everything we see is a gift from Allah.

He gave us metals to use when making cars.

BRIGHTER HORIZONS ACADEMY

He gave us wood, metals, and other building materials to use when making houses and buildings.

He gave us wool, cotton, and material to use when making clothes.

A11

Allah (is) Al-Musawwir

المُصَوِّرُ

THE SHAPER of BEAUTY

Allah made the world beautiful for us.

سورة الحشر

Surah Al-Hashr 59: 24

هُوَ ٱللَّهُ ٱلْخَلِقُ ٱلْبَارِئُ ٱلْمُصَوِّرُ لَهُ ٱلْأَسْمَآءُ ٱلْحُسْنَىٰ يُسَبِّحُ لَهُ مَا فِى ٱلسَّمَوَتِ وَٱلْأَرْضِ وَهُوَ ٱلْعَزِيزُ ٱلْحَكِيمُ ﴿٢٤﴾

TRANSLITERATION

[24] Huwa Allah-ul-khaliq-ul-bari'-ul-musawwiru lah-ul-asma'-ul-husna, yusabbihu lahu mafi-ssamawati wal-'ardi wahuwal-'azeez-ul-hakeem.

TRANSLATION

He is Allah, the Creator, the Inventor, the Shaper. His are the Most Beautiful Names. His purity is proclaimed by all that is in the heavens and the earth, and He is the All-Mighty, the All-Wise. (24)

ALLAH, THE CREATOR

Who made the sun and the sky so blue?
Who made the stars and the planets, too?

Allah is the One, Allah is the One.
Allah made the stars and the moon
and the sun.

Allah is the One. Allah is the One.
Allah, the Creator, the Almighty One.

Who made the flowers and the plants and trees?
Who made the spiders and the honey bees?

Who made the animals, both big and small?
Who made the tiny mouse, the giraffe so tall?

Who made the universe from A to Z?
Who made all the people? Who made you and me?

Listen to this nasheed on Track 2 of your CD.

healthy habit

When you see pretty flowers and plants, be careful not to ruin them. Let others enjoy their beauty, too.

ACTIVITY time

Say "*Subhan'Allah*" every time you see something beautiful or great that Allah made for us.

healthy **habit**

When you look in the mirror and see that Allah has given you a good face and body, say this du'aa':

"اللّهم حَسِّنْ خُلُقي كما حَسَّنتَ خَلْقي"

"Allahuma hassin khuluqi kama hassanta khalqi"

It means: "O Allah, improve my good manners as you have improved my form."

study questions

1 Name five things Allah has given us so that we can live.

2 What should you do when you see a beautiful thing?

3 What are the Arabic names for Allah that mean "The Creator," "The Maker," and "The Shaper of Beauty?"

4 Say the *du'aa'* you say when you see yourself in the mirror.

questions?

1 When do we see the sun? The moon?
2 What happens to the sun when night falls?
3 Whom do we always worship?
4 Who always guides us to the truth?

word watch

[Ibraheem   إبْراهيمْ]

This is the story about our beloved Prophet Ibraheem عليه السلام. He believed in Allah سبحانه وتعالى. He wanted his people to also believe in Allah سبحانه وتعالى.

Let's see what happened.

Ibraheem عليه السلام was a young man in Iraq. He believed in Allah سبحانه وتعالى, but his people did not. This made him very sad. He wanted to show them how they could know about Allah سبحانه وتعالى.

One night, Ibraheem عليه السلام pointed out a shining star to them. It was the biggest and brightest star in the sky. He asked his people, "Do you think this is God? It is the biggest and brightest star in the sky!"

But then the star went away. Ibraheem said, "See? That star is not Allah. Allah سبحانه وتعالى would never go away."

The next thing Ibraheem pointed out was the moon. It was big and bright. He asked his people, "Do you think this could be Allah سبحانه وتعالى ? But, then the moon disappeared. Ibraheem عليه السلام told them, "The moon cannot be Allah, because Allah سبحانه وتعالى would never go away."

Now the night was ending and the people could see the beautiful sun rising in the sky. It was large and bright, and it made them all feel happy. Ibraheem عليه السلام asked them, "Do you think the sun could be Allah?" But everyone remembered that in the evening, the sun set and went away, too. The sun could not be Allah سبحانه وتعالى. Allah always exists. He never sets and never goes away.

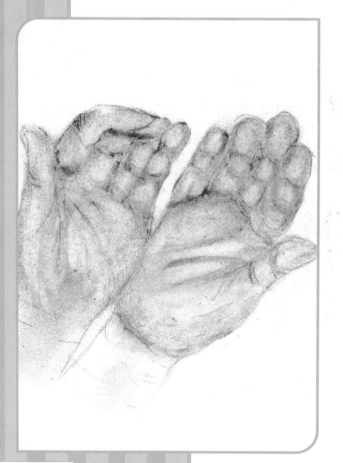

Ibraheem عليه السلام told his people that the star, moon, and sun could never be gods. Only Allah could be God. Allah سبحانه وتعالى guides people to Him if they try to believe in Him. Allah made Ibraheem عليه السلام a prophet who invited people to believe in Allah سبحانه وتعالى.

healthy habit

Always worship Allah alone; do not worship anyone or anything else.

ACTIVITY time

Collect (or draw) pictures of things that remind you that Allah is "*Al-Khaliq*." Stick them on a poster and write "Allah is *Al-Khaliq*" at the top.

study questions

1. Why did the people think the star was Allah سبحانه وتعالى?

2. How did Ibraheem show them that the star, moon, and sun were not Allah سبحانه وتعالى?

3. What did Ibraheem do?

Allah Is One

questions?

1. What is special about Allah?
2. Why is God only One?
3. How is Allah different from us?

word watch

Shahadah شَهادَة
Tawheed تَوْحيد
Al-Asmaa' Al-Husna الأَسْماءُ الحُسْنى

There are five pillars of Islam.
The first pillar of Islam is the *Shahadah*. It is the most important thing that Muslims believe in.
In the *Shahadah*, Muslims say:

لا إله إلا اللّه مُحَمَّدٌ رَسولُ اللّه

"There is no God but Allah. Muhammad is the Messenger of Allah."
The first part of the *Shahadah* says we believe in the one-ness of Allah. The belief in one God is called *Tawheed*.

سورة الإخلاص

Surah Al-Ikhlas 112: 1-4

قُلْ هُوَ ٱللَّهُ أَحَدٌ ۝ ٱللَّهُ ٱلصَّمَدُ ۝ لَمْ يَلِدْ وَلَمْ يُولَدْ ۝ وَلَمْ يَكُن لَّهُۥ كُفُوًا أَحَدٌۢ ۝

TRANSLITERATION

[1] Qul huw-Allahu ahad
[2] Allah-us-samad
[3] Lam yalid walam yoolad
[4] Walam yakul lahu kufuwan ahad

MEANING TRANSLATION

Say, "The truth is that Allah is One. (1) Allah is Besought of all, needing none. (2) He neither begot anyone, nor was he begotten. (3) And equal to Him has never been any one." (4)

Listen to this surah on Track 4 of your CD.

Leena asked her mother one day: "Mama, why is Allah only One?"

Mama: Allah is One because no one can be like Him or does what He can do.

Mama: Allah is only One because there is nothing else like Him. Allah has all the power. No one can be like Him. No one can create the world, the stars, or the sun other than Allah. No one can make people and animals like He can.

Allah has always been here, and He will always be here, forever.
He was never born, and He will never die.
He does not have a mother or a father.
He does not have any children.
Allah never needs anyone to take care of Him.
He never needs any help.
There is only One God, whom we love and worship.

WORDS OF WISDOM
Hadeeth Shareef

حديث شريف

Narrated By At-Tirmithi

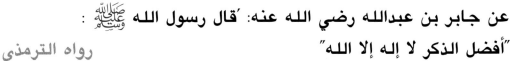

عن جابر بن عبدالله رضي الله عنه: ”قال رسول الله ﷺ :

”أفضل الذكر لا إله إلا الله“   رواه الترمذي

TRANSLITERATION

"Afdal-u-Thikri *La ilaha illa Allah*."

MEANING TRANSLATION

Jabir Ibn Abdullah reported that the Prophet ﷺ said:
"The best way to remember Allah is to say:
"*La ilaha illa Allah*." There is no god but Allah.

healthy
habit

Say: ”لا إله إلا الله“

"*La ilaha illa Allah*."

We say this as many times as we can.

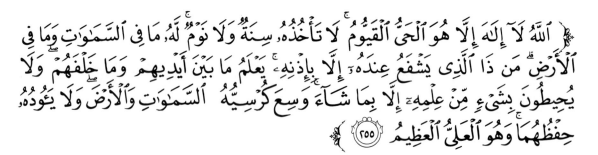

WORDS OF WISDOM

Holy Qur'an

سورة البقرة

Surah Al-Baqara 2: 255

﴿ اللَّهُ لَا إِلَٰهَ إِلَّا هُوَ الْحَيُّ الْقَيُّومُ لَا تَأْخُذُهُ سِنَةٌ وَلَا نَوْمٌ لَّهُ مَا فِي السَّمَاوَاتِ وَمَا فِي الْأَرْضِ مَن ذَا الَّذِي يَشْفَعُ عِندَهُ إِلَّا بِإِذْنِهِ يَعْلَمُ مَا بَيْنَ أَيْدِيهِمْ وَمَا خَلْفَهُمْ وَلَا يُحِيطُونَ بِشَيْءٍ مِّنْ عِلْمِهِ إِلَّا بِمَا شَاءَ وَسِعَ كُرْسِيُّهُ السَّمَاوَاتِ وَالْأَرْضَ وَلَا يَئُودُهُ حِفْظُهُمَا وَهُوَ الْعَلِيُّ الْعَظِيمُ ﴿٢٥٥﴾ ﴾

TRANSLITERATION

[255] Allahu la ilaha illa huwal-hayy-ul-qayyoom,
la ta-khuthuhu sinatuw-wala nawm,
lahu ma fis-samawati wama fil-ard,
man tha-llathee yashfa'u 'indahu illa bi'ithnih,
ya'lamu ma bayna aydeehim wama khalfahum,
wala yuheetoona bishay'in min ilmihi illa bima shaa', wasi'a kursiyyuh-us-samawati wal-ard,
wala ya'ooduhu hifthuhuma.
wahuwa-al-aliyy-ul-atheem.

TRANSLATION

Allah: There is no god but He, the Living, the All-Sustaining. Neither dozing overtakes Him nor sleep. To Him belongs all that is in the heavens and all that is on the earth. Who can intercede with Him without His permission? He knows what is before them and what is behind them; while they encompass nothing of His knowledge, except what He wills. His Kursiyy (Chair) extends to the Heavens and to the Earth, and it does not weary Him to look after them. He is the All-High, the Supreme. (255)

ACTIVITY time

With your friend, make a banner that says:

"لا إله إلا الله"

Hang it on your classroom wall.

لا إله إلا الله

"La ilaha illa Allah."

There is no god but Allah.

Shahadah

La ilaha illa Allah.
Only one God, Allah.
La ilaha illa Allah.
Say *Shahadah*!

Muhammad rasulollah,
Messenger of Allah.
Muhammad rasulollah.
Say *Shahadah*!

La ilaha illa Allah.
Muhammad rasulollah.
La ilaha illa Allah.
Say *Shahadah*!

Listen to this nasheed on Track 5 of your CD.

Allah is One!

Allah has *Al-Asmaa' Al-Husna*, the beautiful names of Allah. There are 99 names. Let us learn some of them:

Allah	is	Al-Wahid	الواحد	→	The One
Allah	is	As Samad	الصمد	→	The Self-Sufficient
Allah	is	Al-Hayy	الحي	→	The Living
Allah	is	Al-Qayyum	القيوم	→	The Self-Existing
Allah	is	Al-Aliyy	العلي	→	The Most High
Allah	is	Al-Atheem	العظيم	→	The Great

study

questions

1 What do we say in the Shahada?

2 What is the best way to remember Allah?

3 What are some names of Allah?

I Love Allah; He Loves Me

questions?

1 Who loves you even more than your parents?
2 How do you know that Allah loves you?
3 Why should you love Allah?
4 How much do you love Allah?

word watch

[*Al-Wadood*   الوَدود
The Loving One]

I love Allah because He loves me, and He gave me life.

I love Allah because He gave me eyes to see things that I love.

He gave me a nose to smell wonderful things.

Allah gave me ears to hear all kinds of wonderful sounds.

He gave me a mouth to smile, talk, and laugh.
I also use my mouth to eat and drink.

Allah gave me the sense of touch. I can feel soft and smooth things. I can feel cool, and I can feel warm.

I love Allah because He loves me, and He takes care of me.

Allah gave me parents and teachers to teach me good things.

He gave me a house to live in, clothes to wear, and food to eat.

Allah gave me water to drink and to clean myself.

He gave me friends to laugh, learn, and play with.

I love Allah because He loves me,
and He made me a Muslim!

Allah gave me
family
and friends.

I Love God; He Loves Me

I love God; He loves me.
I love God; He loves me.
He is our loving Lord.
He is also *Al-Wadood*.

I love God; He loves me.
He gave me my family.
He created me and you.
He made us from head to toe.

I love God; He loves me.
He gave me my eyes to see.
He gave me my tongue to talk,
and gave me my feet to walk.

I love God; He loves me.
He gave me all things I need.
He gave us all kinds of food.
We should always make *sujood*.

He is also *Al-Wadood*.

ALLAH (is) Al-Wadood

الوَدودُ

THE LOVING One

Al-Wadood means The Loving One. People love Allah, and He loves them.

Show Allah that you love Him by doing good things. He will show you that He loves you by giving you gifts in this life and in the next life, *Jannah* (Paradise), insha' Allah.

healthy
habit

Always remember what Allah has given you. Learn to love Him by being a good Muslim! Always say this du'aa':

''اللهم ارزقني حبك وحب من أحبك''

"O Allah, provide me with Your love and the love of everyone that loves You."

ACTIVITY time

1. Make a colorful drawing of the name of Allah in Arabic.

2. Make a colorful drawing of the name of Allah in English.

study
questions

1 Name some things Allah has given us to be thankful for.

2 We can never count how many things Allah has given us. Can you name some more things that are not in this lesson?

3 How can we show Allah that we love Him?

4 How do we know that Allah loves us?

Thank You, Allah

questions?

1 Who made you? Who gave you a family? Who gave you friends?

2 Who do you always remember when you see something special?

3 Do you thank Allah for everything that you see, hear, smell, touch, and taste?

4 What is the best way to thank Allah?

word

ni'am	نِعَمْ
ni'mah	نِعمة
Alhamdulillah	الحَمْدُ لله
thikr	ذِكر
Al-Hameed	الحميد

Allah gave us eyes so that we can see.

Allah gave us a nose to smell and breathe with.

Allah gave us ears to hear and enjoy beautiful sounds.

Allah gave us skin so we can feel things.

Allah gave us a mouth so we can speak, taste, and smile.

These are all gifts and blessings, or *ni'am*, from Allah.

Everything Allah has made is for us to use.

He wants us to be happy.

 **time**

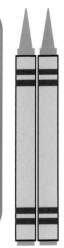

Blink!! Breathe!! Clap!! Smile!!

Now thank Allah that you can do these things.
He has given us the 5 senses.

With our eyes, we see the beautiful world. We see our loved ones, and we see things that we learn about.

With our ears, we hear *Al-Qur'an*, our teachers, our friends, and also *nasheed*.

With our mouths, we speak to each other, eat, and also breathe.

With our hands and legs we work and can feel soft, or smooth, or sticky things.

What would we do without these gifts from Allah?

We must always, always thank Him for them.

WORDS OF WISDOM
Holy Qur'an

سورة التين

Surah At-Tin 95: 1-8

بِسْمِ اللَّهِ وَالتِّينِ وَالزَّيْتُونِ ۝ وَطُورِ سِينِينَ ۝ وَهَذَا الْبَلَدِ الْأَمِينِ ۝ لَقَدْ خَلَقْنَا الْإِنسَانَ فِي أَحْسَنِ تَقْوِيمٍ ۝ ثُمَّ رَدَدْنَاهُ أَسْفَلَ سَافِلِينَ ۝ إِلَّا الَّذِينَ ءَامَنُوا وَعَمِلُوا الصَّالِحَاتِ فَلَهُمْ أَجْرٌ غَيْرُ مَمْنُونٍ ۝ فَمَا يُكَذِّبُكَ بَعْدُ بِالدِّينِ ۝ أَلَيْسَ اللَّهُ بِأَحْكَمِ الْحَاكِمِينَ ۝

TRANSLITERATION

[1] Watteeni wazzaytoon
[2] Wa-toori seeneen
[3] Wa-hath-al-balad-il-ameen
[4] Laqad khalaqna-al-'insana fee ahsani taqweem
[5] Thumma radadnahu asfala safileen
[6] Illa-llatheena amanoo wa'amilos-salihati falahum ajrun ghayru mamnoon
[7] Fama yukaththibuka ba'du biddeen
[8] Alays-Allahu bi-ahkam-il-hakimeen

TRANSLATION

I swear by the Fig and the Olive, (1) And by Tur, the mount of Sinai, (2) And by this peaceful city, (3) We have created man in the best composition, (4) Then We turned him into the lowest of the low, (5) Except those who believed and did righteous deeds, because for them there is a reward never ending. (6) So, what can make you, after all this, to deny the Requital? (7) Is Allah not the Greatest Ruler of all the rulers? (8)

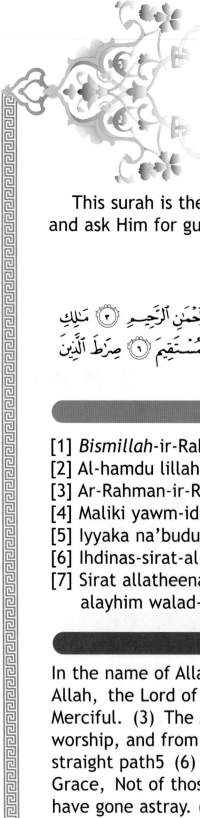

WORDS OF WISDOM
Holy Qur'an

سورة الفاتحة

Surah Al-Fatiha 1: 1-7

This surah is the Opening of the Qur'an. We say it to praise Allah and ask Him for guidance.

بِسْمِ اللَّهِ الرَّحْمَنِ الرَّحِيمِ ﴿١﴾ الْحَمْدُ لِلَّهِ رَبِّ الْعَالَمِينَ ﴿٢﴾ الرَّحْمَنِ الرَّحِيمِ ﴿٣﴾ مَالِكِ يَوْمِ الدِّينِ ﴿٤﴾ إِيَّاكَ نَعْبُدُ وَإِيَّاكَ نَسْتَعِينُ ﴿٥﴾ اهْدِنَا الصِّرَاطَ الْمُسْتَقِيمَ ﴿٦﴾ صِرَاطَ الَّذِينَ أَنْعَمْتَ عَلَيْهِمْ غَيْرِ الْمَغْضُوبِ عَلَيْهِمْ وَلَا الضَّالِّينَ ﴿٧﴾

TRANSLITERATION

[1] *Bismillah*-ir-Rahman-ir-Raheem
[2] Al-hamdu lillahi rabb-il-aalameen
[3] Ar-Rahman-ir-Raheem
[4] Maliki yawm-id-deen
[5] Iyyaka na'budu wa-iyyaka nasta'een
[6] Ihdinas-sirat-al-mustaqeem
[7] Sirat allatheena an'amta alayhim ghayr-il-maghdoobi
  alayhim walad-daalleen

TRANSLATION

In the name of Allah, the Beneficent, the Merciful (1) Praise belongs to Allah, the Lord of all the worlds (2) The All-Merciful, the Very-Merciful. (3) The Master of the Day of Requital. (4) You alone do we worship, and from You alone do we seek help. (5) Take us on the straight path5 (6) The path of those on whom You have bestowed Your Grace, Not of those who have incurred Your wrath, nor of those who have gone astray. (7)

Things we can do to thank Allah:

- **Say** *Alhamdulillah* **and make** *du'aa'*

- **Take care of our bodies and all that He has given us**

- **Pray on time, five times a day**

- **Obey Allah, and do everything He wants us to do**

Allah is Al-Hameed

الحَميدَ

The Praiseworthy

Allah has given us everything we have.
We must always praise Him for every (gift) *ni'mah* He has given us.

healthy

h a b i t

Say   الـحَـمْـد لِـلّه
"*Alhamdulillah*"
when you remember something Allah has created or made for us.

It means: *"All praise is for Allah."*

Praising Allah

■ *Thikr* is one way to thank Allah and remember Him.

■ *Thikr* is done by the heart and the tongue.

■ Saying "*Subhan'Allah, Alhamdulillah, La ilaha illa Allah,* and *Allahu Akbar,*" are kinds of *thikr*.

THIKR

Subhan'Allah.
We praise Allah.

Alhamdulillah.
We thank Allah.

La ilaha illa Allah.
There is no god but Allah.
Allah is One.

Allahu Akbar.
Allah is Great.

Listen to this nasheed on Track 6 of your CD.

ACTIVITY time

1. Choose a partner and look at each other's hands, eyes, mouths, and noses. Talk about these perfect creations that Allah has given us.

2. Do the following things with your friends:
   - Try to use one hand in taking your notebook out of your backpack and write "Allah."
   - Try to draw a house with your eyes closed.
   - Try to ask your friend to give you something without speaking.

Talk about how you feel doing these things, and be thankful to Allah that He has given you hands, eyes, and a mouth.

3. Listen to this *nasheed*: "Thank you, Allah."

study questions

1. Name something that Allah has given you that means a lot to you, something that you really love and thank Allah for. Draw it.

2. What is *thikr*? Give some examples.

3. How do you thank Allah?

I Am a Believer

questions?

1. What do Muslims believe in?
2. How many pillars of faith are there?

word watch

Arkan-ul-Iman	أركان الإيمان
Al-Qadar	القدر
Yawm-ul-Qiyamah	يوم القيامة
Al-Mala'ikah	الملائكة
Al-Kutub	الكتب
Al-Qur'an	القرآن
Al- Anbiyaa'	الأنبياء
war-Rusul	والرسل

Muslims believe in *Arkan-ul-Iman*. Arkan means pillars. Iman means faith, which means to believe in Allah and the unseen world.
Let us learn the pillars of faith. Every Muslim must believe in *Arkan-ul-Iman*.

6 Pillars of Faith أركان الإيمان

الإيمان بالله

1 We Believe in Allah

There is no god but Allah.
He created us and everything in this world.
He is the only One we should worship and pray to.
He has the best Names and Attributes.
No one is like Him.

الإيمان بالملائكة

2 We Believe in Angels, Al-Malai'kah

Angels obey Allah's command.
They protect us and write down our deeds.
They are created from light.
They always obey Allah.
Jibreel, Mika'eel, Israfeel, Ridwan and Malik
are names of great angels .

الإيمان بالكتب

We Believe in the Holy Books, Al-Kutub

The Holy Books are:

1. *As-Suhuf*: Given to Prophet Ibraheem
2. *At-Tawrah*: Given to Prophet Musa
3. *Az-Zaboor*: Given to Prophet Dawood
4. *Al-Injeel*: Given to Prophet Isa
5. *Al-Qur'an*: **Given to Prophet Muhammad** ﷺ

الإيمان بالرسل

We Believe in the Prophets & Messengers, Al-Anbiyaa' War-Rusul

Allah sent many Prophets, but only 25 are mentioned in *Al-Qur'an*. Prophets are the best people that ever lived. We must believe in all the Prophets. We must love them and try to be like them. Prophet Muhammad ﷺ was the last Prophet. We love Prophet Muhammad and Prophets Adam, Nouh, Ibraheem, Musa, Dawood, and Isa, (peace be upon them all).

الإيمان باليوم الآخر

5 We Believe in The Day of Judgment, Yawm-ul-Qiyamah

The Day of Judgment will come after every human, plant, and animal dies.
The Earth and the universe will disappear.
On the Day of Judgment, Allah will make us alive again, all together.
He will ask us about our deeds.
Allah will decide who will go to *Jannah* (Paradise), and who will go to *Jahannam* (Hellfire).

الإيمان بالقَدر

6 We Believe in Al-Qadar

Al-Qadar is Allah's will.
Allah knows everything that is going to happen.
Nothing happens without Allah's permission.
We have to accept everything that happens to us.
If good things happen, we thank Allah.
If bad things happen, we accept them and also praise Allah and say *Alhamdulillah*.
We should trust in Allah, no matter what happens to us. We should also do our best to do what is right.

WORDS OF WISDOM
Holy Qur'an

سورة الكافرون

Surah Al-Kafiroon 109: 1-6

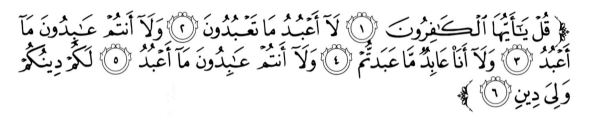

﴿ قُلْ يَـٰٓأَيُّهَا ٱلْكَـٰفِرُونَ ۝١ لَآ أَعْبُدُ مَا تَعْبُدُونَ ۝٢ وَلَآ أَنتُمْ عَـٰبِدُونَ مَآ أَعْبُدُ ۝٣ وَلَآ أَنَا۠ عَابِدٌ مَّا عَبَدتُّمْ ۝٤ وَلَآ أَنتُمْ عَـٰبِدُونَ مَآ أَعْبُدُ ۝٥ لَكُمْ دِينُكُمْ وَلِىَ دِينِ ۝٦ ﴾

TRANSLITERATION

[1] Qul ya ayyuha-alkafiroon
[2] La a'budu ma ta'budoon
[3] Wala antum aabidoona ma a'bud
[4] Wala ana aabidun ma abadtum
[5] Wala antum aabidoona ma a'bud
[6] Lakum deenukum waliya deen

TRANSLATION

Say, "O disbelievers, (1) I do not worship that which you worship, (2) Nor do you worship the One whom I worship. (3) And neither I am going to worship that which you have worshipped, (4) Nor will you worship the One whom I worship. (5) For you is your faith, and for me, my faith." (6)

Listen to this surah on Track 14 of your CD.

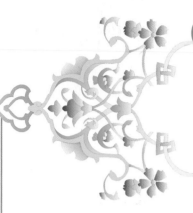

WORDS OF WISDOM
Holy Qur'an

سورة القارعة

Surah Al-Qaria 101: 1-11

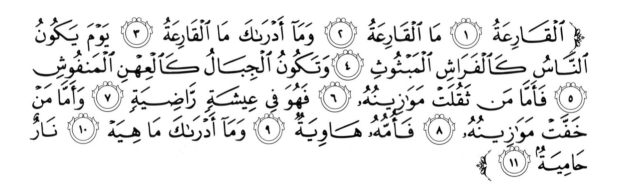

TRANSLITERATION

[1] Alqari'ah

[2] Mal-qari'ah

[3] Wama 'adraaka mal-qari'h

[4] Yawma yakoon-un-nasu kalfarash-il-mabthooth

[5] Watakoon-ul-jibalu kaal'ihn-il-manfoosh

[6] Fa'amma man thaqulat mawazeenuh

[7] Fahuwa fee 'eeshat-ir-radiyah

[8] Wa'amma man khaffat mawazeenuh

[9] Fa'ommuhu hawiyah

[10] Wama adraaka ma hiyah

[11] Narun hamiyah

TRANSLATION

The Striking Event! (1) What is the Striking Event? (2) And what may let you know what the Striking Event is? (3) It will happen) on a day when people will be like scattered moths, (4) And the mountains will be like carded wool. (5)Then, as for him whose scales (of good deeds) are heavy, (6) He will be in a happy life. (7) But he whose scales are light, (8) His abode will be Abyss. (9) And what may let you know what that (Abyss) is? (10) A blazing Fire! (11)

*Listen to this surah on **Track 7** of your CD.*

questions

1 What is the first thing Muslims must believe in?

2 What do angels do?

3 Name some prophets of Allah.

4 On what day will Allah make us alive again after we have died?

5 What does *Al-Qadar* mean?

6 Name three books Allah had sent to mankind?

UNIT B

MY GREAT PROPHET

His Name Was Muhammad

questions?

1. Who was the last prophet?
2. What city did he live in when he was a boy?
3. How much should you love the Prophet?

word watch

Muhammad	مُحَمَّدْ
Makkah	مكة
Madinah	المدينة

One day, Zaid was reading a book. It was about the last Prophet.

Zaid's mom walked into the room.
Mama: What are you reading, Zaid?
Zaid: I am reading a book about the last Prophet.
Mama: Masha'Allah Zaid! Tell me about him.
Zaid: Well, his name was Muhammad ﷺ .
Mama: Sallallahu 'alayhi wasallam. (Peace and blessings of Allah be upon him.)

His name was **Muhammad**

healthy
h a b i t

Always say

صَلَّى اللّٰهُ عَلَيْهِ وَسَلَّم

"sallAllahu 'alayhi wasallam"
when you hear the Prophet's name.

This means: 'Peace and blessings of Allah be upon him.'

Zaid: Allah chose Muhammad to be the last Prophet. Prophet Muhammad taught us good things. He showed us how to be excellent Muslims.

Mama: Yes! Prophet Muhammad ﷺ is the best example for all of us to follow.

Zaid: I love Prophet Muhammad! I want to be like him!

Mama: Where did Prophet Muhammad ﷺ live?

Zaid: He lived in *Makkah* when he was a boy. The people of *Makkah* loved him. Later, when he moved to *Madinah*, people there loved him, too!

Mama: We should love Prophet Muhammad ﷺ too, even more than ourselves!!!

Prophet **Muhammad** ﷺ was:

Patient
Honest
Wise
Kind

MUHAMMAD

We love Muhammad
Oh yes we do.
He is our Prophet
To him we're true.
Blessed *Rasulullah*, it's you!
Muhammad, we love you.

We love Muhammad
sent from Allah.
Was born in *Makkah* to Aminah.
He was the son of Abdullah.
Muhammad from Allah.

We love Muhammad
Called "*Al Ameen*."
He was the greatest man
You've ever seen.
He taught us how to pray
and be clean.
Muhammad *Al Ameen*.

*Listen to this nasheed on **Track 8** of your CD.*

ACTIVITY time

1. Write the name of Prophet Muhammad ﷺ in Arabic and English.

2. Point at *Makkah* and *Madinah* in the map below.

study

questions

1 What should you say when you hear the Prophet's ﷺ name?

2 Can you find *Makkah* on the map?

3 How did the people in *Makkah* feel about the Prophet when he was a boy?

4 Tell us about the manners of Muhammad ﷺ.

Muhammad As a Child

questions?

1. Where was Muhammad ﷺ born?
2. Who were his parents?
3. Who were some of his uncles?
4. Who were some of his cousins?

word watch

Aminah	آمِنَـة
Abdullah	عَبْدُاللَّه
Haleemah	حَلِيمَة
Abdul-Muttalib	عَبْدُالمُطَّلِبْ
Abu-Talib	أبو طالِبْ
Ali	عَلِي
Quraysh	قُرَيْشْ

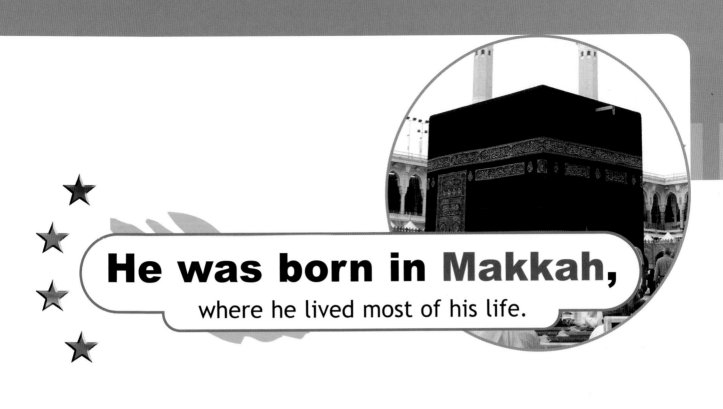

He was born in Makkah,

where he lived most of his life.

His father was Abdullah.

So his name was Muhammad Ibn Abdullah مُحمد بن عبدالله

His mother was Aminah.

When Prophet Muhammad ﷺ was a young boy he lived in the desert of *Makkah*.

His family sent him there to learn pure Arabic and to enjoy the healthy air.

Haleemah As-Sa'diyyah took care of him in the desert. She was a kind and loving lady. She was like a mother to Prophet Muhammad ﷺ . She loved him very much, and he loved her. Her family was also very nice to him.

His grandfather was Abdul-Muttalib.

Abu Talib, Hamzah, and Al-Abbas were his uncles.

Some of his cousins were Ali Ibn Abi Talib, Ja'far Ibn Abi Talib, Abdullah, and Ibn Abbas.

Muhammad ﷺ was from the tribe of

Quraysh قُرَيْش

People of his tribe lived in *Makkah*. They used to travel to other places to buy and sell things.

They used to travel from *Makkah* to Yemen in the wintertime...

... and from *Makkah* to Syria in the summertime.

WORDS OF WISDOM
Holy Qur'an

سورة قريش

Surat Quraysh 106

بِسْمِ اللَّهِ الرَّحْمَٰنِ الرَّحِيمِ

لِإِيلَٰفِ قُرَيْشٍ ۝ إِۦلَٰفِهِمْ رِحْلَةَ الشِّتَاءِ وَالصَّيْفِ ۝ فَلْيَعْبُدُواْ رَبَّ هَٰذَا الْبَيْتِ ۝ الَّذِىٓ أَطْعَمَهُم مِّن جُوعٍ وَءَامَنَهُم مِّنْ خَوْفٍۭ ۝

TRANSLITERATION

[1] Li-'eelafi Quraysh

[2] Eelafihim rihlat-ashshitaa'i-wassayf

[3] Fal-ya'budoo rabba hatha-lbayt

[4] Allathee 'at'amahum min joo'iw-wa-amanahum min khawf

TRANSLATION

Because of the familiarity of the Quraish, (1) that is, their familiarity with the trips of winter and summer, (2) they must worship the Lord of this House, (3) who gave them food against hunger, (4) and gave them security against fear

Listen to this surah on Track 8 of your CD.

Prophet Muhammad's father died before he was born.
His mother died when he was still a very young boy.
Prophet Muhammad was an orphan.

PROPHET MUHAMMAD WAS ALWAYS

when he was young and also when he was old.

The Prophet's grandfather and uncles took great care of him.
They loved him and kept him safe.

study

questions

1. What city did the Prophet ﷺ live in when he was a child?

2. Who were his parents? What happened to them?

3. Who did the Prophet ﷺ live with in the desert?

4. What was the name of his tribe?

Muhammad Worked Hard

questions?

1 What was Muhammad's ﷺ first job?
2 How did Muhammad ﷺ treat animals?
3 How did Muhammad ﷺ treat other people?

word watch

As-Sadiq Al-Ameen الصَّادِقُ الأمينْ
shepherd راعي
merchant تاجِر

When he was just a boy, Muhammad ﷺ was a shepherd. He took good care of sheep. He was kind to all animals.

Muhammad's ﷺ first job was as a shepherd!!!

Muhammad's ﷺ second job was as a merchant!!

When he was a young man, Muhammad ﷺ became a **merchant**. He traveled to places like Syria to buy, sell, and trade things.

Muhammad ﷺ was always kind and honest. People loved him very much, and they called him *As-Sadiq Al-Ameen*. This means the Truthful and the Trustworthy.

He helped the poor and the needy people.

He solved problems between people and helped them stop fighting.

He was kind to everyone. He made people happy.

Everyone loved and trusted Muhammad ﷺ.

**healthy
habit**

Always be honest, tell the truth, and be kind to all people.

سورة الضحى

Surah Ad-Dhuha 93: 1-11

بِسْمِ اللّٰهِ الرّٰحْمٰنِ الرّٰحِيمِ

وَالضُّحٰى ﴿١﴾ وَاللَّيْلِ إِذَا سَجٰى ﴿٢﴾ مَا وَدَّعَكَ رَبُّكَ وَمَا قَلٰى ﴿٣﴾ وَلَلْأٰخِرَةُ خَيْرٌ لَّكَ مِنَ الْأُولٰى ﴿٤﴾ وَلَسَوْفَ يُعْطِيكَ رَبُّكَ فَتَرْضٰى ﴿٥﴾ أَلَمْ يَجِدْكَ يَتِيمًا فَأٰوٰى ﴿٦﴾ وَوَجَدَكَ ضَاآلًّا فَهَدٰى ﴿٧﴾ وَوَجَدَكَ عَاآئِلًا فَأَغْنٰى ﴿٨﴾ فَأَمَّا الْيَتِيمَ فَلَا تَقْهَرْ ﴿٩﴾ وَأَمَّا السَّآئِلَ فَلَا تَنْهَرْ ﴿١٠﴾ وَأَمَّا بِنِعْمَةِ رَبِّكَ فَحَدِّثْ ﴿١١﴾

TRANSLITERATION

[1] Wadduha
[2] Wallayli itha saja
[3] Ma wadda'aka rabbuka wama qala
[4] Walal-'aakhiratu khayrul-laka min-al-'oola
[5] Walasawfa yu'teeka rabbuka fatarda
[6] Alam yajidka yateeman fa'aawa
[7] Wawajadaka dallan fahada
[8] Wawajadaka 'aa-ilan faaghna
[9] Fa'ammal-yateema fala taqhar
[10] Wa'ammas-sa'ila fala tanhar
[11] Wa'amma bini'mati rabbika fahaddith

TRANSLATION

I swear by the forenoon, (1) And by the night when it becomes peaceful, (2) Your Lord (O Prophet,) has neither forsaken you, nor has become displeased. (3) Surely the Hereafter is much better for you than the present life. (4) And of course, your Lord will give you so much that you will be pleased. (5) Did He not find you an orphan, and give you shelter? (6) And He found you unaware of the way (the Shari'ah), then He guided you. (7) And He found you in need, then made you need-free. (8) Therefore, as for orphan, do not oppress him, (9) And as for the beggar, do not scold him. (10) And about the bounty of your Lord, do talk. (11)

healthy
h a b i t

Always work hard to help your family and others as the Prophet ﷺ did.

ACTIVITY time

Draw a sheep like the ones Prophet Muhammad ﷺ used to herd!

study

questions

1. What was Prophet Muhammad's ﷺ first job?

2. What was his second job? What did he do?

3. How did Prophet Muhammad ﷺ help people?

4. Did people trust Muhammad ﷺ? What did they call him?

The Prophet's Family

questions?

1. Who was the Prophet's ﷺ first wife?
2. Did the Prophet ﷺ have children? How many?
3. How did the Prophet ﷺ treat his family?

word watch

[Ahlul-Bayt آل البَيْت
Khadeejah خَديجَة]

When Prophet Muhammad ﷺ was a merchant, he worked for a great woman named Khadeejah رضي الله عنها. Prophet Muhammad ﷺ was a hard and honest worker. Khadeejah liked his good manners. Later, they got married.

Muhammad ﷺ had four daughters.

1 زَيْنَبْ
Zaynab

2 رُقَيَّـة
Ruqayyah

3 أُمُّ كَلْثومْ
Ummu Kulthoom

4 فاطِمَةُ
Fatimah

He had three sons, but they died when they were young children.

1 القاسِمْ
Al-Qasim

2 عَبْدُاللّه
Abdullah

3 إِبْراهيمْ
Ibraheem

All of the Prophet's ﷺ children died while he was alive, except Fatimah. The Prophet ﷺ was sad, but patient.

Khadeejah رضي الله عنها was the mother of all the Prophet's children except Ibraheem. Ibraheem's mother was Mariyah رضي الله عنها.

After Khadeejah died, Prophet Muhammad ﷺ felt very sad. Later, he married other great women, like Sawdah, A'ishah, and Safiyyah.

The Prophet ﷺ had two grandsons: Al-Hasan and Al-Hussain. They were the children of Fatimah and her husband, Ali ibn Abi Talib, the cousin of Prophet Muhammad ﷺ .

We should love and respect the whole family of the Prophet. They are called *"Ahlul-Bayt"*

The Prophet ﷺ loved his grandsons, and he played with them often. Muhammad ﷺ loved all children very much, and he took special care of them.

WORDS OF WISDOM

Hadeeth Shareef

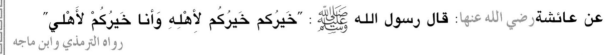

Narrated By Ubn Majah & At-Tirmithi

عن عائشة رضي الله عنها: قال رسول الله ﷺ : "خَيرُكم خَيرُكُم لأهلِهِ وَأنا خَيرُكُمْ لأهلي"
رواه الترمذي وابن ماجه

TRANSLITERATION

"Khayrukum Khayrukum Li-'ahlih, Wa-'ana Khayrukum Li Ahli."

TRANSLATION

"The best among you is the one who is best to his family, and I am the best of you to my family."

study

questions

1. What was the name of Muhammad's ﷺ first wife?

2. How many sons did the Prophet ﷺ have? How many daughters did he have? How many children did he have all together?

3. What were the names of the Prophet's ﷺ children?

4. Which child of the Prophet lived the longest?

5. What were the names of the Prophet's grandchildren?

6. How did Muhammad ﷺ treat his grandsons and other children?

Muhammad Becomes a Prophet

questions?

1. When did Muhammad ﷺ become a Prophet?
2. Where did the Prophet receive the first *ayat* of the Qur'an?
3. Who brought *Al-Qur'an* to Muhammad ﷺ from Allah?

word watch

Jabal-un-Noor	جَبَلْ النورْ
Ghar Hiraa'	غارْ حِراءْ
Jibreel	جِبْريلْ
ayah	آيَـة
ayaat	آياتْ
nabiyy	نبيّ
Rasul	رسول
Rasulullah	رسول الله

- Prophet Muhammad ﷺ used to go to a cave called Ghar Hiraa'. *Ghar Hiraa'* was at the top of a mountain called *Jabal-un-Noor*, or the Mountain of Light.

- He used to stay in *Ghar Hiraa'* for several nights at a time.

- There he would think about the world and the one God who made it so beautiful.

One night, when Muhammad ﷺ was 40 years old, something strange and wonderful happened in Ghar Hiraa', during the month of *Ramadan*.

Muhammad ﷺ was visited by

the ANGEL JIBREEL!!

The Angel Jibreel is the leader of all angels. Allah has created angels out of light. They are kind, gentle, and strong, and they have great faith. They obey Allah all the time. They do whatever Allah tells them to do. They love people. The Angel Jibreel taught Prophet Muhammad ﷺ *Al-Qur'an*. He always told Muhammad ﷺ what Allah wanted him to do.

The Angel Jibreel said to Muhammad ﷺ, "READ."

إقـرأ

Muhammad ﷺ did not know how to read, and he said, "I can't read!"
The Angel Jibreel repeated, "READ!"
Muhammad ﷺ again said, "I can't read!"
Then the Angel Jibreel recited the first *ayaat* (verses) Prophet Muhammad ﷺ heard of *Al-Qur'an*. These were the first five *ayat* of *Surat Al-'Alaq*.

Muhammad now became a *nabiyy*, or prophet.
Allah chose him to teach people the religion of Islam.
Rasul is another word for prophet. It means messenger.
Rasulullah means "Messenger of Allah." Muhammad ﷺ taught people the Message, or Book of Allah.

Muhammad ﷺ was very scared in the cave. He was alone in the cave, and it was dark.
This was the first time that he had seen an angel!

Muhammad ﷺ ran home to tell Khadeejah رضي الله عنها what had happened. Khadeejah made him feel better. She told him that Allah would take care of him because he was such a patient and nice person.

WORDS OF WISDOM
Holy Qur'an

سورة العلق

Surah Al-Alaq 96: 1-19

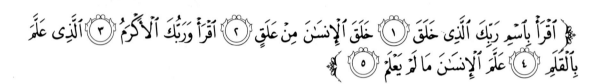

﴿ اقْرَأْ بِاسْمِ رَبِّكَ الَّذِي خَلَقَ ﴿١﴾ خَلَقَ الْإِنْسَانَ مِنْ عَلَقٍ ﴿٢﴾ اقْرَأْ وَرَبُّكَ الْأَكْرَمُ ﴿٣﴾ الَّذِي عَلَّمَ بِالْقَلَمِ ﴿٤﴾ عَلَّمَ الْإِنْسَانَ مَا لَمْ يَعْلَمْ ﴿٥﴾ ﴾

TRANSLITERATION

[1] Iqra' bismi rabbik-allathee khalaq
[2] Khalaq-al-insana min alaq
[3] Iqra' warabbuk-al-akram
[4] Allathee allama bilqalam
[5] Allam-al-insana ma lam ya'lam

TRANSLATION

Read with the name of your Lord who created (every thing), (1) He created man from a clot of blood. (2) Read, and your Lord is the most gracious, (3) Who imparted knowledge by means of the pen. (4) He taught man what he did not know. (5)

Listen to this surah on Track 11 of your CD.

DO YOU KNOW THE MESSENGER

Do you know the Messenger?
The Messenger, the Messenger?
Do you know the Messenger, the Prophet of Allah?

Yes! We know the Messenger,
The Messenger, the Messenger.
Yes! We know the Messenger, the Prophet of Allah.

Do you know the Messenger,
The Messenger, the Messenger?
Do you know the Messenger? Allah gave him Qur'an.

Yes! We know the Messenger,
The Messenger, the Messenger.
Yes! We know the Messenger. Allah gave him Qur'an.

Do you know the Messenger, the Messenger, the Messenger?
Do you know the Messenge? The world will know his fame.

Yes! We know the Messenger,
The Messenger, the Messenger.
Yes! We know the Messenger. The world will know his fame.

Do you know the Messenger, the Messenger, the Messenger?
Do you know the Messenger?
Muhammad is his name.

Yes! We know the Messenger, the Messenger, the Messenger?
Yes! We know the Messenger.
Muhammad is his name.

Listen to this Nasheed on Track 10 of your CD.

WORDS OF WISDOM
Hadeeth Shareef

حديث شريف

Narrated By Al-Bukhari

عن عثمان بن عفان رضي اللّه عنه: أن رسول اللّه ﷺ قال:

"خَيرُكُمْ مَنْ تَعَلَّمَ القُرآنَ وَعَلَّمَهُ."

رواه البخاري

TRANSLITERATION

"Khayrukum man ta'allam-al-Qur'ana wa allamah."

TRANSLATION

Othman Ibn Affan reported that the Prophet ﷺ said: "The best among you is the one who learns the Qur'an and teaches it to others."

healthy
h a b i t

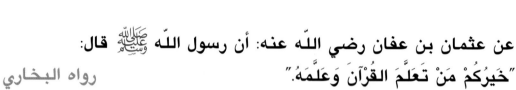

Learn to read the Qur'an and memorize it every day.

ACTIVITY time

Create a poster that has pictures of the *Makkah*, *Jabal-un-Noor*, and the Qur'an.

study

questions

1 Where did Muhammad ﷺ go to think about the world?

2 Who was Jibreel?

3 What was the first word Jibreel said to Muhammad ﷺ?

4 Where did Muhammad ﷺ go after he met Jibreel?

5 What did Khadeejah say to make Muhammad ﷺ feel better?

6 Why do you think Muslims gave *Jabal-un-Noor* this name?

7 Why do you think the first word of the Qur'an was "Read?"

Sahabah, Friends of the Prophet

questions?

1 Who were the friends of the Prophet ﷺ ?
2 Why do you think they loved *Rasulullah* ﷺ ?
3 What does the word *Sahabah* mean?
4 What did they do for him?

word watch

sahabah	صَحابة
sahabi	صَحابي
sahabiyyat	صَحابيّاتْ
Abu-Bakr As-Siddeeq	أبو بَكرْ الصِّديقْ
'Omar Ibn Al-Khattab	عُمَرْ بنْ الخَطّابْ
'Othman Ibn 'Affan	عُثْمانْ بنْ عَفّانْ
'Ali Ibn Abi-Talib	عَلي بِنْ أبي طالِبْ

The Prophet ﷺ had many friends.

His BEST friend was:

أبو بَكرْ الصِّديقْ
'Abu-Bakr
As-Siddeeq

The Prophet's friends, or companions, are known as the
Sahabah. *Sahabah* صَحَابَة is plural for *sahabi* صَحَابِي
A *sahabi* is a friend of Prophet Muhammad ﷺ.

Some of his other friends were:

عُمَرْ بِنْ الْخَطَّاب
'Omar
Ibn-ul-Khattab

رضي الله عنه

عُثْمانْ بِنْ عَفَّانْ
'Othman
Ibn Affan

رضي الله عنه

عَلي بِنْ أَبي طالِب
'Ali
Ibn Abi Talib

رضي الله عنه

Other friends of the Prophet:

- Zaid Ibn Harithah زيد بن حارثة رضي الله عنه was very special to the Prophet ﷺ.
- Bilal Ibn Rabah بلال بن رباح رضي الله عنه gave the first *athan*, and he was the mu'athin.
- Khalid Ibn-ul-Waleed خالد بن الوليد رضي الله عنه was a great leader of the Muslim army.
- Osama Ibn Zaid أسامة بن زيد رضي الله عنه was the youngest Muslim general; he was 17 years old.
- Mus'ab Ibn Omair مصعب بن عمير رضي الله عنه was a great young teacher of Islam.
- Ja'far Ibn Abi-Talib جعفر بن أبي طالب رضي الله عنه was the Prophet's cousin.

They helped the Prophet ﷺ teach Islam to people all the time.
They helped him in *Makkah*. They helped him in *Madinah*.

THE SAHABAH ARE MY HEROES!

The female companions of the Prophet ﷺ are called *sahabiyyat*.

Some of his *Sahabiyyat* were:

خَوْلَة	نُسَيْبَة	أَسْماءْ
Khawlah	**Nusaybah**	**Asmaa'**
Bint-ul-Azwar	Bint Ka'b (Ummu Amarah)	Bint Abu Bakr
رضي الله عنها	رضي الله عنها	رضي الله عنها

All the *sahabah* and *sahabiyyat* LOVED the Prophet ﷺ very much.

healthy

h a b i t

We should love all the *sahabah* and *sahabiyyat*.
Whenever you say the name of a *sahabi*, say:

رَضِيَ اللّه عـنْـه   "RadiyAllah Anhu."

If she is a woman you say:

رَضِيَ اللّه عـنْـها   "RadiyAllah Anha."

This means: "May Allah be pleased with him or her"

Allah loved as-*sahabah* because they were excellent Muslims.
Allah said that He is pleased with them and promised them *Jannah*.

s t u d y

•—questions—

1. What do we call the friends of the Prophet ﷺ?

2. What were some of the names of the *sahabah*?

3. Who was Muhammad's ﷺ best friend?

4. Where did the *sahabah* help the Prophet ﷺ?

5. What did Allah say about the *sahabah*?

6. What can we do to follow the example of the *sahabah*?

B39

UNIT C

WORSHIPPING ALLAH

Arkan-ul-Islam, The Five Pillars of Islam

questions?

1 What are somethings that ALL Muslims must do?
2 How many pillars of Islam do you know?
3 How many pillars of Islam do you practice?

word watch

Arkan-ul-Islam	أرْكانُ الإسْلامْ
Shahadah	شَهادَة
salah	صَلاة
Al-Ka'bah	الكعبة
sawm	صَوْمْ
siyam	صِيامْ
Ramadan	رَمَضانْ
zakah	زَكاة
Hajj	حج

Muslims come from many places, but they practice the same acts of worship.

All Muslims believe in the five pillars of Islam, *Arkan-ul-Islam*.

Arkan-ul-Islam

**1** The first pillar is the Shahadah.

The *Shahadah* is the Muslim statement of faith. It is said in Arabic:

أشهد أن لا إله إلا الله
وأشهد أن محمدا رسول الله.

"Ash'hado an *La ilaha illa Allah* wa ash'hado anna Muhammadan ﷺ *rasulullah*."

This means that you believe in only one God, Allah. It means also that Muhammad ﷺ is the Messenger of Allah. We say the *Shahadah* in every prayer and in our du'aa'.

Allah alone created us, and He created *Rasulullah* to be our role model. He taught us what is right and wrong.

healthy habit

Say the *Shahadah* as many times as you can. You will get many *hasanat* every time you say it.
This means that we believe in only one God, Allah, and that Muhammad is the Messenger of Allah.

C3

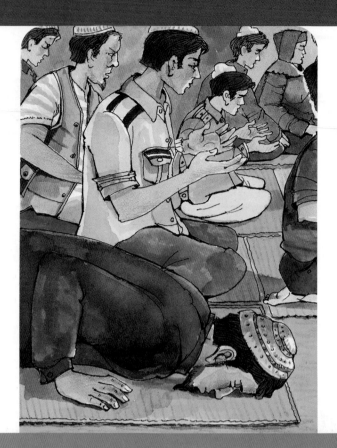

 **The second pillar is Salah.**

Salah means prayer. Muslims pray to Allah five times a day. No matter where we are, we pray to Allah. We face the direction of *Al-Ka'bah* in *Makkah*. Prayer is a way for us to show Allah that we love Him. During *Salah* we thank Him for all His gifts. Allah says:

''وأقيموا الصلاة''

Wa aqeemossalah
(And offer prayer)

healthy

h a b i t

Learn how to do *Salah*, and always pray on time.

3 The third pillar is Sawm or Siyam.

Muslims fast during the days of the month of *Ramadan*. We fast by not eating or drinking, from dawn until sunset. We also try to be on our best behavior. Fasting can make you hungry. This lets you feel how poor people feel every day.

Fasting teaches you to control yourself by not eating or drinking when you are hungry or thirsty.

"يا أيها الذين آمنوا كتب عليكم الصيام كما كتب على الذين من قبلكم لعلكم تتقون."

"Ya ayyuha-llatheena amanoo kutiba alaykum-us-siyamu kama kutiba ala-llatheena min qablikum la'allakum tattaqoon."

O you who believe! Fasting is prescribed to you as it was prescribed to those before you, that you may be mindful of God.

Al-Baqarah - *Ayah* 183

healthy habit

Learn how to fast, and try to fast the whole month of *Ramadan*.

4 The fourth pillar is Zakah.

Zakah is charity, money that we give to help the poor. Muslims should always help out others when they can. One way to help the poor is by giving them money.

Allah says:

''وآتوا الزكاة''

Wa atozzakah
(And give *Zakah*)

healthy
h a b i t

Give charity to the poor when you have extra money. If you do not have money, smile at people. Prophet Muhammad taught us that smiling is charity too.

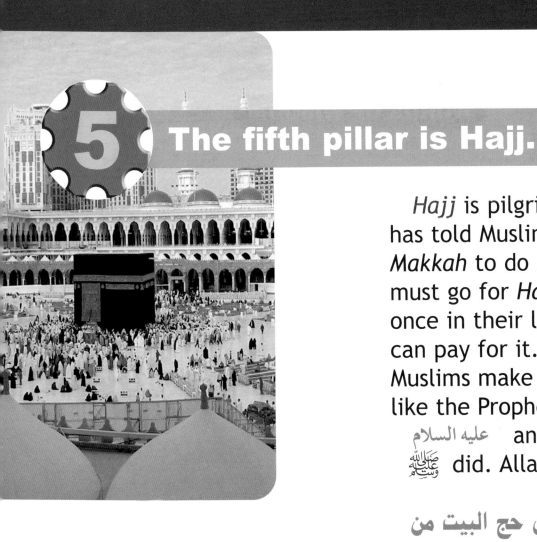

5 The fifth pillar is Hajj.

Hajj is pilgrimage. Allah has told Muslims to go to *Makkah* to do *Hajj*. Muslims must go for *Hajj* at least once in their lifetime if they can pay for it. In *Makkah*, Muslims make a pilgrimage like the Prophets Ibraheem عليه السلام and Muhammad ﷺ did. Allah says:

"ولّه على الناس حج البيت من استطاع إليه سبيلا"

"Wa lillahi Alan-Nasi Hijj-ul-bayti man istataa'a Ilayhi Sabeela."

(And (due) to Allah from the people is a pilgrimage to the House - for whoever is able to find thereto a way.)

Al-'Imran - *Ayah* 97

healthy habit

At the time of *Hajj*, watch a movie or read a book about *Hajj*, and have your parents explain *Hajj* to you.

WORDS OF WISDOM

(Hadeeth Shareef)

حديث شريف

Narrated by Muslim & Bukhari

عن ابن عمر رضي اللّه عنه: قال رسول اللّه ﷺ :

بُنِي الإسلام على خمس: شهادةِ أن لا إله إلا اللّه وأن محمداً رسول اللّه وإقامِ الصَّلاةِ وإيتاءِ الزكاةِ وصومِ رمضانَ وحجٍّ البيت"

رواه البخاري ومسلم

TRANSLITERATION

"Boniya-Al-Islamu ala Khams, Shahadati an la ilaha illa-Allah wa anna Muhammadan *Rasulullah* wa Iqami-*Salah*, wa ita'i-*Zakah*, wa sawmu *Ramadan* wa *Hajj*-ul-Bayt."

TRANSLATION

Ibn Omar رضي الله عنه reported that the Prophet ﷺ said: "Islam is built on five pillars; to witness that there is no God but Allah, and Muhammad is the Messenger of Allah, to do the prayers, to give charity, to fast *Ramadan*, and to go to *Hajj* (if you can go there)."

The **5** Pillars of Islam

The first pillar is the Shahadah.

The second pillar is Salah.

The third pillar is Sawm or Siyam.

The fourth pillar is Zakah.

The fifth pillar is Hajj.

Pillars Of Islam

One, One, only One,
Only God Allah.
These are the pillars of Islam.
Only God Allah.

Pray, pray, pray *salah*.
Pray five times a day.
These are the pillars of Islam.
Pray five times a day.

Fast, fast, fast all day,
Fast in *Ramadan*.
These are the pillars of Islam.
Fast in *Ramadan*.

Give, give, give zakat.
Give to help the poor.
These are the pillars of Islam.
Give to help the poor.

Round, round, round we go
When we make the *Hajj*.
These are the pillars of Islam.
Make our pilgrimage.

Listen to this Nasheed on Track 12 of your CD.

ACTIVITY time

Draw a *masjid* that has five pillars, and write the name of one pillar of Islam on each pillar of the *masjid* you draw.

study

questions

1 Can you count how many times a day you say the *Shahadah* during *Salah*?

2 Where do you face when you pray? And how many times should a Muslim pray every day?

3 In what month do Muslims practice the fourth pillar (*Sawm*)?

4 Who does *Zakah* help?

5 How many times must a Muslim make *Hajj*? Where do Muslims go for *Hajj*?

I Love Salah, Prayer

questions?

1. What is the key to *Jannah*?
2. How can we be with *Rasulullah* ﷺ in *Jannah*?
3. What are the names of the five daily prayers?

word watch

Fajr	فَجْرْ
Thuhr	ظُهـرْ
Asr	عَصْرْ
Maghrib	مغْرِبْ
Isha'	عِشاءْ

One day, Zaid saw his father praying. When his father finished, Zaid asked him:

Zaid: Baba, why do we pray?

Follow the Prophet's way;
pray 5 times a day!

Baba: Allah ﷻ created us to worship Him. When we pray, we worship Him and show our love for Him ﷻ.

When we love Allah ﷻ, Allah loves us even more. He gives us happiness in this life, and *Jannah* in the life after.

Also, when we pray, we thank Allah ﷻ for everything He has given us.

Zaid: Wow, doing our *salah* brings us so many good things! I used to think that it was hard to pray so many times, but now I know that Allah has told us to pray because it is GOOD for us!

Baba: Yes, Zaid. Keeping up with your prayers will take you somewhere special. *Listen to this story:*

Storytime

Once a young *sahabi* (a friend of the Prophet ﷺ) named Rabi'ah bin Ka'b, asked to be with the Prophet in *Jannah*. Rabi'ah was 14 years old. The Prophet ﷺ asked him,

"Is there anything else you want, Rabi'ah?" Rabi'ah answered, "No. All I want is to be with you in *Jannah*." The Prophet ﷺ said:

‏‏''أَعِنِّي عَلَى نَفْسِكَ بِكَثْرَةِ السُّجُودِ''‏

"Then help yourself by making plenty of *Sujood*." Narrated by Muslim

Zaid: So *salah* will even help us be with *Rasulullah* ﷺ in *Jannah*!

Do you know what the key to *Jannah* is?

Prayer is the key to Paradise!!

Baba asked Zaid: Now, do you know what the five daily prayers are?

Zaid: Let me think...*Fajr*, *Thuhr*, *Asr*, *Maghrib*, and **Isha'**!

Baba: Very good! Now do you know when we do these prayers?

Zaid: I think I need some help here.

Baba smiled: Of course. Let's go through them together.

Fajr

We pray *Fajr* before the sun rises in the morning.

Thuhr

We pray *Thuhr* in the early afternoon, after lunchtime.

ASR

We pray *Asr* in the late afternoon, when the sun is a little low in the sky.

MAGHRIB

We pray *Maghrib* right after the sun sets.

Isha'

We pray *Isha'* at night, before we go to sleep.

WORDS OF WISDOM
Hadeeth Shareef

حديث شريف

Narrated By Muslim & Bukhari

عن عبدالله بن مسعود رضي الله عنه قال: سألت النبي ﷺ:
أي العمل أحب إلى الله؟ قال: الصلاة على وقتها."

رواه البخاري ومسلم

TRANSLITERATION

Abdullah Ibn Mas'ood (R): Ayyul 'Amali Ahabbu IlAllah?
The Prophet ﷺ said: "As-salatu ala waqtiha."

TRANSLATION

Abdullah Ibn Mas'ood asked the Prophet ﷺ , "What is the good deed that Allah loves the most?" The Prophet ﷺ answered, "Praying right on time."

SALAH

A Muslim prays five times a day.
Salah, salah.
A Muslim prays five times a day.
Salah, salah.
A Muslim prays five times a day
To keep the cursed *Shaitan* away.
And we all bow down to pray
Each day, five times a day.
Pray, pray, pray, pray,
Pray, pray, pray, pray.

At *Fajr* we awake to pray *salah, salah.*
At *Fajr* we awake to pray *salah, salah.*
At *Fajr* we awake to pray
The perfect way to start each day.

At *Thuhr* once again we pray *salah, salah.*
At *Thuhr* once again we pray *salah, salah.*
At *Thuhr* once again we pray.
We eat our lunch then go to pray.

At *Asr* time we stop and pray *salah, salah.*

At *Asr* time we stop and pray *salah, salah*.
At *Asr* time we stop and pray.
We put aside our toys and pray.

At *Maghrib* when the sun goes down, *salah, salah*.
At *Maghrib* when the sun goes down, *salah, salah*.
At *Maghrib* when the sun goes down
We place our heads upon the ground.

Isha before we go to bed *salah, salah*.
Isha before we go to bed *salah, salah*.
Isha before we go to bed
We pray then rest our sleepy heads.

A Muslim prays five times a day.
Salah, salah.
A Muslim prays five times a day.
Salah, salah.
A Muslim prays five times a day
To keep the cursed *Shaitan* away.
And we all bow down to pray
Each day, five times a day.
Pray, pray, pray, pray,
SALAH!!

Listen to this Nasheed on Track 15 of your CD.

time

Salah Tracker

Make a chart like this to help you keep track of your prayers:

Prayer	MON	TUES	WED	THURS	FRI	SAT	SUN
Fajr	✔	✔					
Thuhr	✔	✔					
Asr	✔	✔					
Maghrib	✔						
Isha	✔						

study

questions

1. Why do we pray to Allah? Give three reasons.

2. What can you do to be with the Prophet ﷺ in *Jannah*?

3. What is the first prayer of the day? What is the last prayer?

4. What is the prayer right after sunset?

5. Can you draw a Muslim praying?

Wudoo' Makes Me Clean

questions?

1 What should we do before doing prayers?
2 What body parts do we clean when we make wudoo'?
3 What should you say before and after you make wudoo'?
4 Can *Wudoo'* be broken? What breaks your wudoo'?

word watch

niyyah	نِيَّة
Wudoo'	وُضوءْ
taharah	طَهارَة

سورة المائدة

Surah Al-Maeda 5:6

بِسْمِ اللَّهِ الرَّحْمَٰنِ الرَّحِيمِ

﴿ يَٰٓأَيُّهَا ٱلَّذِينَ ءَامَنُوٓا۟ إِذَا قُمْتُمْ إِلَى ٱلصَّلَوٰةِ فَٱغْسِلُوا۟ وُجُوهَكُمْ وَأَيْدِيَكُمْ إِلَى ٱلْمَرَافِقِ وَٱمْسَحُوا۟ بِرُءُوسِكُمْ وَأَرْجُلَكُمْ إِلَى ٱلْكَعْبَيْنِ ۝ ﴾

PARTIAL TRANSLITERATION

"Ya ayyuha-allatheena amanoo itha qumtum ila-assalati faighsiloo wujoohakum wa-aydiyakum ila-almarafiqi wamsahoo biru'oosikum wa-arjulakum ila-alka'bayn."

TRANSLATION

O you who believe, when you rise for Salah, (prayer) wash your faces and your hands up to the elbows, and make Mash (wiping by hands) of your heads and (wash) your feet up to the ankles...(6)

Allah told us to be in a state of *taharah* before *salah*. *Taharah* (cleanliness) means to be in a state of purity. Our *salah* won't count if we have not cleaned certain parts of our body. The action of cleaning these parts is called **wudoo'**. So we must make *Wudoo'* whenever we pray. Let's go through *Wudoo'* step by step!

healthy
h a b i t

When you enter the bathroom, say your du'aa:

اللَهمَ إِنِّي أَعوذُ بِكَ مِنَ الخُبْثِ والخَبَائِثْ

"Allahumma inni a'oothu bika minal kubuthi wal kabaa'ith"

It means: "Oh Allah, protect me from dirt and devils."
Remember to step in with your LEFT foot first!
When you are done, step out with your right foot!

This is how Dad taught me to make wudoo':

1 I make my *niyyah*. I say in my mind what I am about to do. Here, my *niyyah* is to make wudoo'.

2 I say "*Bismillah*," which means "in the name of Allah." This reminds us that we are making *Wudoo'* for Allah.

3 Then, I wash my hands THREE times up to my wrists. This reminds me to do only good things with my hands.

4 After that, I rinse out my mouth THREE times using my right hand. I use my mouth to eat and talk. So, I should eat only good things and say only nice words.

5 Then, I rinse the inside of my nose and blow it using my left hand THREE times. This reminds me to be thankful to Allah for giving me a sense of smell.

6 After that, I wash my face THREE times. I make sure water cleans my face from the hair on my forehead down to my chin, and from my right ear to the left ear.

7 Then, I wash my arms all the way up to my elbows THREE times. I wash my right arm before my left arm. The Prophet ﷺ told us to do good things with our right hands.

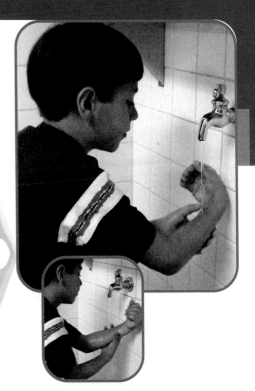

8 Then, I wet my hands a little, and wipe my head from the front to the back. Then I bring my hands back to the front again. I do this once.

9 Then, I gently wipe the inside and the back of my ears with some more water. This teaches me to listen only to good things.

10 Now I am ready to wash my feet. I wash both feet up to my ankles THREE times. I wash my RIGHT foot FIRST. I make sure the water gets between my toes and cleans any dirt that may be there. Cleaning my feet helps me remember to go to good places.

Now we are done making wudoo'! *Allahu Akbar!* Now, I say the *Shahadah.*

"أشهد أن لا إله إلا الله وأشهد أن محمدا رسول الله"

Ash-hadu an *La ilaha illa Allah*, Wa Ash-hadu anna Muhammadan *Rasulullah!*

I bear witness that there is no god but Allah, and I bear witness that Muhammad is the Messenger of Allah

حديث شريف

Narrated By Ahmad & At-Tirmithi

عن ابن عامر رضي الله عنه: أن رسول الله ﷺ قال:
"من توضأ فأحسن الوضوء فقال أشهد أن لا إله إلا الله وحده لا شريك له وأن محمدا عبده ورسوله فتحت له ثمانية أبواب من الجنة يدخل من أيها شاء."

رواه الترمذي وأحمد

TRANSLITERATION

"Man Tawadda'a fa-ahsan-alwudoo'a faqala ash-hadu an la ilaha ill-Allah wahdahu la shareeka lahu wa anna Muhammadan Abduhu wa rasooluhu futihat lahu thamaniyatu abwabin min al-*Jannah* yadkhulu min ayyuha shaa'."

TRANSLATION

"He who performs *Wudoo'* perfectly, and then recites the *Shahadah*, will have the eight gates of *Jannah* open for him (on the Day of Judgment) to enter through any one he wishes."

healthy

habit

Always have your Wudoo', so you will be ready to pray all the time!

Wudoo'

This is the way we make *Wudoo'*
Make wudoo', make wudoo'.
This is the way we make *Wudoo'* before we say our prayer.

This is the way we wash our hands,
wash our hands, wash our hands.
This is the way we wash our hands
When we make our wudoo'.

This is the way we wash our mouth,
wash our mouth, wash our mouth.
This is the way we wash our mouth
When we make our wudoo'.

This is the way we wash our nose,
wash our nose, wash our nose.
This is the way we wash our nose
When we make our wudoo'.

This is the way we wash our face,
wash our face, wash our face.
This is the way we wash our face
When we make our wudoo'.

This is the way we wash our arms,
wash our arms, wash our arms.
This is the way we wash our arms
When we make our wudoo'.

This is the way we wash our head,
wash our head, wash our head.
This is the way we wash our head
When we make our wudoo'.

This is the way we wash our feet,
wash our feet, wash our feet.
This is the way we wash our feet
When we make our wudoo'.

Now we are Muslims nice and clean,
nice and clean, nice and clean.

Now we are Muslims nice and clean
To stand in front of Allah.

Listen to this Nasheed on Track 16 of your CD.

Things That Break Your *Wudoo'*

You must remember that some things can break your wudoo'! If you:

■ use the restroom
■ pass gas
■ fall asleep

you must make *Wudoo'* **again** before you pray.

healthy
habit

1. When you are in the bathroom, remember that you should:
   - keep yourself clean
   - keep the bathroom clean
2. Try not to talk when you are in the bathroom.
3. When you leave the bathroom, step out with your RIGHT foot and say:

"Ghufraanak"    ''غُـفْـرانَك''

It means: (O, Allah, I want) your forgiveness.

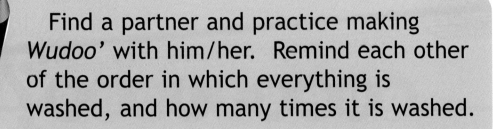

ACTIVITY time

Find a partner and practice making *Wudoo'* with him/her. Remind each other of the order in which everything is washed, and how many times it is washed.

study
questions

1 List parts of your body that are washed in wudoo'.

2 What parts are washed only ONCE?

3 What do you say before and after you make your wudoo'?

4 What side do you start each step with? Why?

5 What things can break your wudoo'?

6 What *du'aa'* do you say when entering and leaving the restroom?

Zaid Learns How to Pray

questions?

1. What are the different movements in *salah*?
2. Where do we face when we pray?
3. Does every prayer have the same number of *rak'at*?

word watch

qiyam	قِيامْ
rukoo'	رُكوعْ
sujood	سُجودْ
juloos	جُلوسْ
tasleem	تَسْليمْ
rak'ah	رَكْعَة
rak'at	رَكَعات
Qiblah	قِبْلَة
fard	فَرْضْ
Tashahhud	تَشَهُّدْ
Assalatul Ibraheemiyyah	الصَّلاةُ الإبراهيمِيَة
hasanat	حسنات

Zaid knew his birthday was coming up. He was going to turn seven! But there was something more important than turning seven. Zaid was going to learn how to pray! Zaid ran to Dad.

Zaid asked: "Dad, can you teach me how to make *salah*?"
Dad said: " Of course, Zaid. Let's learn *salah* together! Remember, first you have to make wudoo'!"

Zaid made wudoo', and Dad began to teach Zaid how to pray.

Salat al-*Fajr*

1 You face the **Qiblah** and make *niyyah* (intention) in your heart. *Niyyah* is knowing what you are about to do and why you are doing it. You should always make sure you pray and do all good deeds for Allah.

What is the Qiblah, Dad?

The Qiblah is the direction you face when you pray. It is toward *Al-Ka'bah*, in *Makkah*.

C35

2 You raise your hands behind your ears and say

اللّهُ أُكْـبَـرْ

"Allahu Akbar" (Allah is Greater).

3 While you are standing, you put your right hand over your left hand by your belly bottom. This is called *qiyam*. You read *Surat-ul-Fatihah* and a short surah or few ayat.

4 You say الله أُكْبَـر , "*Allahu Akbar*," then make *rukoo'*. *Rukoo'* is when you bow down and put both hands on your knees.

5 During *rukoo'* you say سُبحانَ ربي العظيم "Subhana Rabiyal Atheem" (Glory to my Lord the Great) THREE times.

6 You rise from *rukoo'* and say سَمِعَ اللّه لِمنْ حمده، ربنا ولك الحمد "Sami'a-Allahu Liman Hamidah" (Allah hears those who praise Him). Then, you say "Rabbana Wa Lak-Al-Hamd" (Our Lord, praise be to You.)

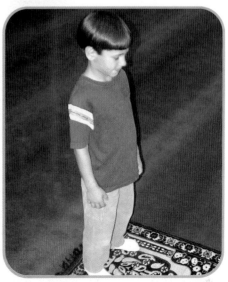

7 You say اللّهُ أُكْـبَـرُ , then make *sujood* by resting your forehead, nose, hands, knees and toes on the floor. You say سُبْحان رَبِّي الأعلى , "Subhana Rabiyal Ala'ala" (Glory be to the Most High (Allah]) THREE times.

8 You sit up from *sujood* while saying اللّهَ أُكْـبَـرُ . Then repeat *sujood* again.

You just completed one full *rak'ah*!! A *rak'ah* is made up of *qiyam*, 1 *rukoo'*, and 2 *sujood*!

9 To start the second *rak'ah*, you stand up saying اللّهَ أُكْـبَـرُ , from *sujood*, and repeat steps 3 to 8 .

10 After you finish the second *rak'ah*, you sit down (*juloos*) to read At-*Tashahhud* and As-Salatul Ibraheemiyyah.

ACTIVITY time

Practice two *rak'at* with your classmates.

التشهُّد
At-*Tashahhud*

التحيات لله والصلوات والطيبات،
السلام عليك أيها النبي ورحمة الله وبركاته،
السلام علينا وعلى عباد الله الصالحين،
أشهد أن لا إله إلا الله وحده لا شريك له،
وأشهد أن محمدا عبده ورسوله.

At-Tahayyatu lillahi wassalawatu wattayyibat, Assalamu 'alay-ka 'ayyuhan-nabiyyu warahmatullahi wabarakatuh, Assalamu 'alayna wa 'ala ibad-illahis-saliheen, Ashahadu 'alla 'ilaha illAllah wahdahu la sharica lah wa 'ash-hadu anna Muhammadan 'abduhu wa rasooluh

All compliments, all physical prayer,
and all monetary worship are for Allah.
Peace be upon you, Oh Prophet,
and Allah's mercy and blessings.
Peace be on us and on all righteous slaves of Allah.
I bear witness that no one is worthy of worship except Allah
And I bear witness that Muhammad is His slave and Messenger.

الصَّلاة الإبراهيمية
As-Salatul Ibraheemiyyah

اللهم صلِّ على محمد وعلى آل محمد
كما صليت على إبراهيم وعلى آل إبراهيم
وبارك على محمد وعلى آل محمد
كما باركت على إبراهيم وعلى آل إبراهيم
في العالمين، إنك حميد مجيد.

Allahumma salli 'ala Muhammad wa 'ala aali Muhammad
Kama sallayta 'ala Ibraheem wa 'ala aali Ibraheem
wa barek 'ala Muhammad wa 'ala aali Muhammad
Kama barakta 'ala Ibraheem wa 'ala aali Ibraheem
Fi-l'aalameen, innaka hameedun majeed

All compliments, all physical prayer,
and all monetary worship are for Allah.
Peace be upon you, Oh Prophet,
and Allah's mercy and blessings.
Peace be on us and on all righteous slaves of Allah.
I bear witness that no one is worthy of worship except Allah,
And I bear witness that Muhammad is His slave and Messenger.

11 You turn your face to the right side and say:
" السلام عليكم ورحمة الله " ,
"*Assalamu Alaykum wa Rahmatu-Llah*" (Peace and Mercy of Allah be upon you).

12 You turn your face to the left side and say the same.
This is called *tasleem*.

Zaid was so happy to learn how to make *Salah*!!!

Zaid had another question.

Zaid: Dad, I know that we have to do 5 *fard* (required) prayers every day; *Fajr*, *Thuhr*, Asr, *Maghrib*, and Isha. Are the *rak'at* the same for all the prayers?

Dad: Excellent question, Zaid. The number of *rak'at* for some of these *fard* prayers is not the same. They can have 2 or 3 or 4 *rak'at*.

Zaid: I know how to pray 2 *rak'at*, because you just taught me that. But how about 3 and 4 *rak'at*?

Dad: Well, for *Maghrib*, you have three *rak'at*. The first 2 *rak'at* are like *Fajr* salat, except you go back into qiyaam after your *Tashahhud*. The last *rak'ah* will be normal, but you don't read a short surah after Al-Fatihah. Then in *juloos*, you say your *Tashahhud* and As-Salatul Ibraheemiyyah, and end with *tasleem*.

Let's remember this:

■ *Fajr*	2 *rak'at*
■ *Thuhr*	4 *rak'at*
■ **Asr**	4 *rak'at*
■ *Maghrib*	3 *rak'at*
■ **Isha**	4 *rak'at*

Zaid: How about 4 *rak'at*?

Dad: For 4 *rak'at* prayers, you do your first two *rak'at* like *Fajr*, but you get up after the *tashahhud*. You repeat the same steps for the next 2 *rak'at*. You just need to remember that you don't read a short surah after **Al-Fatihah** in the third and forth *rak'at*.

Zaid: How am I going to remember all this, Dad?!

Dad: The more you practice, the easier it will get. Don't worry, son, I will help you. I know you can do it, insha Allah!

In a few days, Zaid said to Dad:

Zaid: Dad, *Salah* is so much easier now! The more I pray to Allah, the more I love it!

Dad: I knew you would do a great job in your *salah*, Zaid. I am very proud of you. Today, I bought you a present; it is a prayer rug.

Zaid: Oh, Jazak Allah khayran Dad; I love you.

Zaid enjoyed every *salah* he made after that. He thanked his father for teaching him and for the great present. He also knew Allah would give him *hasanat*, or good deeds.

ACTIVITY time

Practice a 3 *rak'at* prayer and a 4 *rak'at* prayer with your classmates. Have your teacher or parent watch you.

healthy habit

Always pray your *salah* on time!!

study
questions

1 What movements is one *rak'ah* made of?

2 Where is the Qiblah?

3 What should you say in your heart before you pray?

4 How many *rak'at* are in *Fajr* prayer? How about *Thuhr*, Asr, *Maghrib* and Isha?

5 Draw a picture of a Muslim child doing *qiyam*, rukoo', *sujood*, and *juloos*.

questions?

1 What is *Ramadan*?
2 What do Muslims do in *Ramadan*?
3 Do you love *Ramadan*?

word watch

Ramadan	رمضان
siyam	صيام
taraweeh	تراويح
iftar	إفطار
suhoor	سُحور
ajr	أجر
Ar-Rayyan	الريان

Ramadan is a very special month for Muslims.
It is the month of *siyam*, fasting.

Siyam is one of the five pillars of Islam.
Muslims around the world love *Ramadan*.
They do many good things in this month.
They fast from *Fajr* (dawn) to *Maghrib* (sunset) every day
of *Ramadan*.

Muslims read more Qur'an in *Ramadan*.
They have long prayers called *taraweeh* every night.
They give food and money to the poor.

Families invite each other to *iftar*, which is a dinner to break the fast at sunset.
They also wake up very early to eat *suhoor*.
Suhoor is a meal they eat before *Fajr* to help them fast the whole day.
We enjoy cooking food for our families, especially in *Ramadan*.

Children also go to the *masjid* and pray.
They listen to lessons about Islam.
They learn Qur'an and memorize it.

Children also fast in *Ramadan*.
If you are seven, try to fast the whole
day. If you can't, fast for half a day.
The first time can be hard, but you will
get used to it.

We learn many lessons in *Ramadan*.
We learn how the poor and hungry people feel.
We learn self-control when we see yummy food, but
we do not eat it.
We learn great manners.
We learn to say and hear good things, like the Qur'an,
thikr, *du'aa'* and *nasheed*. And we avoid saying or lis-
tening to bad words.
We learn to see good things, and not to watch bad
things.

Allah gives us great *ajr*, or reward, for fasting in
Ramadan.
Allah gives *Jannah* to those who fast in *Ramadan*.
Muslims who fast enter *Jannah* through a gate called
Ar-Rayyan.

NASHEED

Ramadan

In Blessed *Ramadan*
A Muslim fasts for thirty days.
In Blessed *Ramadan*.
To Allah we give thanks and praise.
In Blessed *Ramadan*.

In Blessed *Ramadan*
We wake and eat before the dawn.
In Blessed *Ramadan*
We eat *suhoor*; the day is long.
In Blessed *Ramadan*.

In Blessed *Ramadan*
We fast until the sun goes down.
In Blessed *Ramadan*
Our families all will gather round.
In Blessed *Ramadan*.

In Blessed *Ramadan*
We savor each delicious bite.
In Blessed *Ramadan*
We pray together every night.
In Blessed *Ramadan*.

In Blessed *Ramadan*
The fast is done and *Eid* is here.
In Blessed *Ramadan*
Can't wait to fast again next year.

Listen to this Nasheed on Track 17 of your CD.

WORDS OF WISDOM
Hadeeth Shareef

حديث شريف

Narrated By Al-Bukhari & Muslim

عن أبي هريرة رضي الله عنه: قال رسول الله ﷺ :
"إذا جاء رمضان فتحت أبواب الجنة، وغلِّقت أبواب النار، وصُفدت الشياطين."

رواه البخاري ومسلم

TRANSLITERATION

"Itha Ja'a *Ramadan*, futihat abwab-ul-Jannaj, wa-Ghulliqat abwab-un-Nar wa suffidat-ishyateen."

TRANSLATION

Abu Hurayrah رضي الله عنه reported that Rasoolullah ﷺ said: "When *Ramadan* comes, the gates of *Jannah* open, the gates of Hell close, and Satan will be locked up."

healthy
habit

Try to fast as many days as you can in the blessed month of *Ramadan*.

Muslims do not say bad words, especially in *Ramadan*.
They do not hurt others in *Ramadan* and all other times.
They forgive each other if they have fights.

study

questions

1 What is *siyam*?

2 When do Muslims fast in *Ramadan*?

3 What do Muslims do during *Ramadan*?

4 What is *iftar*? What is *suhoor*?

5 What does Allah give to people who fast in *Ramadan*?

6 What lessons do we learn in *Ramadan*?

UNIT D

MY MUSLIM WORLD

My Muslim Brothers and Sisters

questions?

1. What country do you live in? What city?
2. Do you have friends or family in other cities? How about in other countries?
3. What are three places in the world that are special to all Muslims?

word watch

ummah	أُمَّـة
akh	أَخْ
ukht	أُخْـتْ

MUSLIMS come in all different colors and looks.

Muslims are all brothers and sisters in Islam.
We are all one *ummah*. An *ummah* is the community of Muslims.

Allah made the world for us
to live together,
in love and peace.

Muslims live ALL OVER THE WORLD!!!
We are all brothers and sisters in Islam!!!

Muslims share many things

All Muslims believe in one God, Allah ﷻ . They follow the same prophet, Muhammad ﷺ

All Muslims pray toward one Qiblah, *Al-Ka'bah*, in *Makkah*. Muslims go to *Makkah* for *Hajj*, all wearing the same thing.

Allah loves it when Muslims pray in jama'ah.
All Muslims are equal in front of Allah.

All Muslims love the three holy cities: *Makkah*, *Madinah*, and *Al-Quds* (Jerusalem). Allah made very interesting things happen at these three places a long time ago. That is why they are special. We will learn all about these cities later.

Did you know that there are more than 1 BILLION and a half Muslims in the world?

أخ (*akh*) in Arabic means "brother"

Wow! I have more than a billion brothers and sisters in Islam! That is great. I don't even think I can count that high!

أخت (*ukht*) in Arabic means "sister"

There are over 50 Muslim countries.

Egypt

Indonesia

Somalia

Pakistan

Muslims live in many different places.

Muslims live in Spain and France

Muslims live in India

Muslims live in China

Muslims Live in the United States

There are **seven million Muslims** in the United States.

There are around **2100 mosques** in America.

A mosque in Tempe, Arizona, USA.

All the Muslims in the world make up

the **Muslim ummah**

We  all our brothers and sisters around the world.

WORDS OF WISDOM
Holy Qur'an & Hadeeth Shareef

قرآن كريم
وحديث شريف

١) ﴿ إِنَّمَا ٱلْمُؤْمِنُونَ إِخْوَةٌ ﴾   سورة الحجرات، آية ١٠

٢) ﴿ إِنَّ هَٰذِهِۦ أُمَّتُكُمْ أُمَّةً وَٰحِدَةً وَأَنَا۠ رَبُّكُمْ فَٱعْبُدُونِ ٩٢ ﴾
سورة الأنبياء، آية ٩٢

٣) "المسلم أخو المسلم" رواه البخاري ومسلم عن عبدالله بن عمر رضي الله عنه

TRANSLITERATION

1. "Innamal-Mu'minoona Ikhwah"
2. "Inna hathihi Ummatukum ummataw-wahidataw-wa-ana rabbukum fa'budoon"
3. "Al-Muslimu *Akh*-ul-Muslim"

TRANSLATION

1. "Believers are brothers." 49:10
2. " Your nation is one, and I am your Lord, so worship Me." 21:92
3. "The Muslim is a brother to another Muslim."

A Hadeeth reported by Abdullah Ibn Umar in Al-Bukhari and Muslim

ACTIVITY time

Collect pictures of 10 mosques from different countries around the world.
Stick them on a poster board.

study

questions

1 Do Muslims live in Japan? How about Canada? Mexico? Russia? Germany?

2 Name some Muslim countries.

3 How many Muslims live in the world?

4 What are some things that all Muslims share?

5 What do we call the Muslim community in the world?

6 How would you say "brother" and "sister" in Arabic?

questions?

1. How should you greet another Muslim?
2. Why do Muslims say *Assalamu Alaykum*? And what does it mean?
3. When do Muslims say *Assalamu Alaykum*?

word watch

Assalamu Alaykum   السَّلام عَليكُم
Wa Alaykum Assalam   وعَليكُم السَّلام

Assalamu Alaykum!
That means "Peace be Upon You!"
We say this whenever we meet a
Muslim, and when we leave a Muslim!

السَّلامُ عَلَيْكُم

This is the Muslim greeting.

We say

السَّلام عليكُم

"Assalamu Alaykum"

to our family when we wake up in the morning, and when we go to sleep at night.

We say

السَّلام عليكُم

"Assalamu Alaykum"

when we see our friends and teachers at school, and when we leave them to go home.

We say

السَّلام عليكُم

"Assalamu Alaykum"

when we meet Muslims at a store.

We say

السَّلام عليكُم

"*Assalamu Alaykum*"

to our brothers and sisters at the *masjid* before and after prayers.

We say

السَّلام عليكُم

"*Assalamu Alaykum*"

to our family when we come home.

and they all say:

وعليكُم السَّلام

"wa alaykum assalam!"

That means, "Peace be upon you, too!"
It gives us so many good deeds!

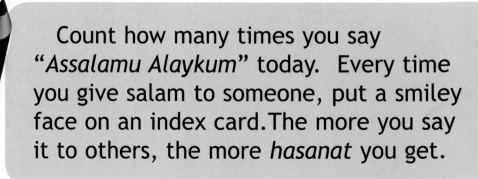

Count how many times you say "*Assalamu Alaykum*" today. Every time you give salam to someone, put a smiley face on an index card. The more you say it to others, the more *hasanat* you get.

Allah (is) As-Salam

السَّلامُ

↓

The Source of Peace

Allah gives peace to the world. We should always wish peace upon the people around us by saying, "*Assalamu Alaykum.*"

healthy
habit

Always say السَّلام عليكُم
"*Assalamu Alaykum*" when you see another Muslim.   Remember to say "wa alaykum assalam" if someone says "*Assalamu Alaykum*" to you first.

Storytime

10

20

30

Once the Prophet ﷺ was sitting with his companions, when a man came to the group and said, "*Assalamu Alaykum.*"

The Prophet ﷺ answered, "Wa Alaykum Assalam, ten."

Then another man came and joined the group, saying "*Assalamu Alaykum* **wa Rahmatullah**."

The Prophet ﷺ answered, "Wa alaykum assalaam wa Rahmatullah, twenty."

Then a third man came and said, "*Assalamu Alaykum* wa Rahmatullahi **wa Barakatuh**."

The Prophet ﷺ replied, "Wa alaykum assalam wa Rahmatullahi wa Barakatuh, thirty."

When the *sahabah* asked why he said those numbers, *Rasulullah* ﷺ said that you get 10 *hasanat* when you say, "*Assalamu Alaykum.*" However, you get 20 *hasanat* if you say, "*Assalamu Alaykum* wa Rahmatullah." Best of all, you get 30 *hasanat* if you say, "*Assalamu Alaykum* wa Rahmatullahi wa Barakatuh."

THIS MEANS WE SHOULD ALWAYS SAY THE LONGEST GREETING TO GET THE MOST HASANAT!

Muslims all over the world say

السَّلامُ عَليكُم

"Assalamu Alaykum!"

People say "hello," "hi," "hey," and "what's up" when they meet. They also say "bye" when they leave each other. It is better for Muslims to say "*Assalamu Alaykum*." This has a very good meaning and gives Muslims many *hasanat* every day. It also makes Muslims love each other more.

Assalamu Alaykum

Assalamu Alaykum,
Wa alaykum assalaam.
This is how you greet your dad,
and how you greet your mom.

Assalamu Alaykum,
Wa alaykum assalam.
Smile at your friends and
teachers, as you walk along.

Assalamu Alaykum
Wa alaykum assalam.
Say this to all the Muslims, and
together we'll be strong!

WORDS OF WISDOM
Hadeeth Shareef

حديث شريف

Narrated by Muslim

عن أبي هريرة رضي الله عنه: قال رسول الله ﷺ قال:

"أفشو السلام بينكم" رواه مسلم

TRANSLITERATION

"Afshos Salama baynakum."

TRANSLATION

Abu Hurayrah رضي الله عنه the Prophet ﷺ said:
"Spread the greeting of *Assalamu Alaykum* among you."

study

questions

1 What does "*Assalamu Alaykum*" mean?

2 Which is better, to say "Hi" or "*Assalamu Alaykum*" when you meet or leave other Muslims? Why?

3 If someone says "*Assalamu Alaykum*" to you, how should you reply?

4 Name some places where you meet Muslims.

5 How can you get more *hasanat* when you greet others?

questions?

1. What holidays do you celebrate?
2. How many times a year do you have this holiday?
3. What do you do on this day?

word watch

Eid al-Fitr	عيد الفِطرْ
Eid al-Adha	عيدُ الأضْحى
Hajj	حج
Thul Hijjah	ذو الحجة
takbeer	تكبير
udhiyah	أُضْحِيَة
khutbah	خُطْبَة

Muslims

CELEBRATE EID

twice a year.

The FIRST Eid is عيد الفطر

Eid al-Fitr

Muslims celebrate *Eid al-Fitr* for three days after fasting the month of *Ramadan*. We know it is *Eid* when we see the new moon.

The SECOND Eid is عيد الأضحى

Eid al-Adha

Muslims celebrate *Eid al-Adha* in the month of **Thul-Hijjah**, during the time of *Hajj*. The celebration lasts for four days. On this *Eid*, Muslims make *udhiyah*, or sacrifice. They share the *udhiyah* meat with friends, family, and the poor.

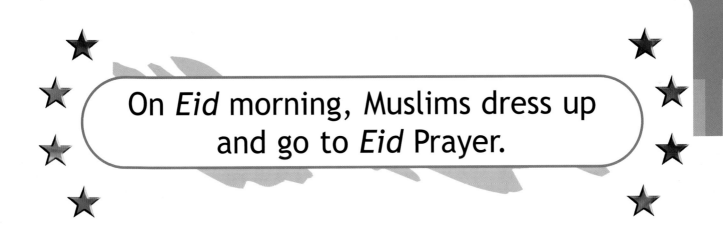

On *Eid* morning, Muslims dress up and go to *Eid* Prayer.

1. They say the *Eid* takbeer together,

2. They pray two *rak'at* of Salat-ul-*Eid*.

3. Then they listen to a special *Eid* khutbah, or speech.

4. Then everyone hugs and says:

عيد مُبارَك

Eid Mubarak!!!

Takbeer of Eid

اللّه أَكْبَرْ، اللّه أَكْبَرْ، اللّه أَكْبَرْ، لا إله إلاّ اللّه

Allahu Akbar, Allahu Akbar , Allahu Akbar.
La ilaha illa Allah.
This means: Allah is the Greatest, Allah is the Greatest, Allah is Greater. There is no god but Allah.

اللّه أَكْبَرْ، اللّه أَكْبَرْ، ولِلّهِ الحَمْد

Allahu Akbar, Allahu Akbar, Wa lillah Alhamd.
This means: Allah is the Greatest, Allah is the Greatest, and praise be to Allah.

Children receive gifts and money

Eid Mubarak

When *Ramadan* comes to an end
The crescent moon is sighted
All Muslims wait with joy and then -
Eid Mubarak!

We wake and rise before the dawn
Get ready for our prayer
Our brand new clothes we now put on.
Eid Mubarak!

A time of joy, a time of peace
Our families all will gather
To start the *Eid al-Fitr* Feast.
Eid Mubarak!

We greet our friends throughout the day
With many hugs and handshakes
To everyone we meet we say
Eid Mubarak!

The party starts, come join the fun
With candy, toys and presents
There's something nice for everyone.
Eid Mubarak!

A time of joy, a time of peace
Our families all will gather
To start the *Eid al-Fitr* Feast
Eid Mubarak!

And when the days of *Eid* are done,
Give thanks again to Allah
For blessing each and everyone.
Eid Mubarak!

Eid Mubarak EVERYONE!

Listen to this nasheed on Track 18 of your CD.

Allah loves us.
He gave us *Eid* so we can celebrate and be happy.

Families visit each other and eat yummy food

REMEMBER

There are Muslims in the world who don't get a wonderful *Eid*. Sometimes they don't have enough food to eat or money to buy *Eid* gifts. We should always be generous and give others as much as we can, so all Muslims can have a beautiful *Eid*.

ACTIVITY time

1. Draw a picture of what you do on *Eid*.
2. Sit with your friends and say the *takbeer* of *Eid* together.

study
questions

1   How many times a year do Muslims celebrate *Eid*?

2   What are the names of the two Eids?

3   How long is *Eid al-Fitr*?
What about *Eid al-Adha*?

4   What do Muslims do after the *Eid* prayer?

5   What special things do Muslims do on *Eid al-Adha*?

6   What is fun about *Eid*?

Beautiful Makkah, the Holiest City

questions?

1. If you could go anywhere in the world, where would you go?
2. Where do you face when you pray?
3. What are some special things about *Makkah*?

word watch

Hajj	حَجْ
Al-Ka'bah	الكَعْبَة
Makkah	مَكَّة
Al-Masjid al-Haram	المَسْجِدُ الحَرامْ
Zamzam	زمْزَمْ
Ghar Hiraa'	غار حراء
Jabal-un-Noor	جبل النور

Do you know the name of the most special city for Muslims?

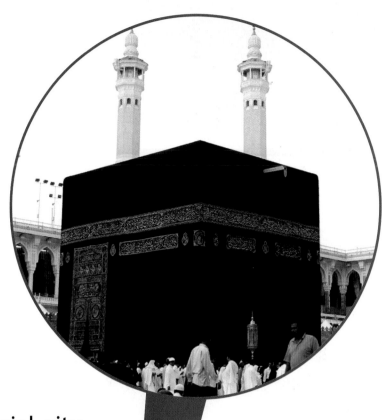

Makkah is the most special city for all Muslims.

It is in a Muslim country called Saudi Arabia.

Prophet Adam عليه السلام and his family lived in *Makkah* and died there.
They were the first family that lived on Earth.

Much later, Prophet Ibraheem عليه السلام and his son, Prophet Isma'eel عليه السلام , built *Al-Ka'bah* in *Makkah*. This was many, many years before Prophet Muhammad ﷺ was born.

Ghar Hira'

Prophet Muhammad was born in *Makkah*, more than 1400 years ago.

He became a prophet in *Makkah*. *Al-Qur'an* was revealed to him there.
Muhammad ﷺ received the first *ayat* of *Al-Qur'an* in *Ghar Hiraa'* on the top of *Jabal-un-Noor*, or the Mountain of Light.

Jabal-un-Noor, or the Mountain of Light

Makkah was very special to Prophet Muhammad ﷺ. Abu Bakr, Omar, Othman, Ali, and many of the first Muslims were born and lived in *Makkah*. Later, they moved to Madina with the prophet ﷺ.

All Muslims pray to the direction of *Al-Ka'bah*. *Al-Ka'bah* is in *Al-Masjid al-Haram*. This means "The Sacred Mosque."

Next to *Al-Ka'bah* in *Al-Masjid al-Haram* is the well of *Zamzam*. A well is a deep hole in the ground, filled with water. This well has holy water in it. Allah made this spring of water for Prophet Isma'eel and his mother thousands of years ago.

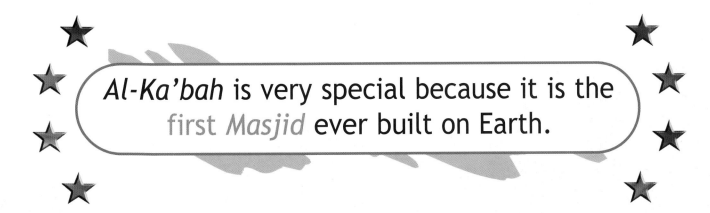

Al-Ka'bah is very special because it is the first *Masjid* ever built on Earth.

Praying in *Al-Masjid al-Haram* gives us 100,000 times more rewards than praying anywhere else in the world. One day you will visit *Al-Ka'bah* and pray near it, insha'Allah!

D38

ACTIVITY time

Remember that you face *Al-Ka'bah* in *Makkah* when you pray. Muslims in India, Syria, China, Brazil, America, and everywere else in the world face the same place when they pray. Think about how special it is for all the Muslims in the world to pray toward the same place, five times a day.

Draw the Ka'bah, and hang your art in your room.

study

questions

1. What is the most special city for Muslims?

2. Where is *Makkah*?

3. Who were the first people in *Makkah*?

4. Who built *Al-Ka'bah*?

5. Why was *Makkah* special to Prophet Muhammad ﷺ?

6. Why is the spring of *Zamzam* special? Where in *Makkah* is it?

Al-Madinah, the City of Light

questions?

1. Where is Prophet Muhammad's ﷺ *masjid*?
2. Why did the first Muslims leave *Makkah* and go to Al-*Madinah*?
3. What other special things do you know about Al-*Madinah*?

word watch

Al-Madina Al-Munawwarah	المَدينَة المُنَوَّرة
Yathrib	يَثْرِب
Al-Masjid An-Nabawi	المَسْجِدُ النَّبَوِي
Al-Baqea'	البقيع

Al-Madinah is another city in Saudi Arabia.

It is the second holiest city for Muslims.

Why is *Madinah* so special?

When the new Muslims were not treated nicely in *Makkah*, they moved to Al-*Madinah*. Madina was a safer place for them. At that time, the city was called *Yathrib*.

Prophet Muhammad's ﷺ *masjid* is in Al-*Madinah*. It is called *Al-Masjid An-Nabawi*. This means "The mosque of the Prophet."

The early Muslims built the *masjid*, and Prophet Muhammad's ﷺ house was next to it.

Prophets are usually buried where they die. When Prophet Muhammad ﷺ died, he was buried in his house, next to the *masjid*.

Prophet Muhammad's ﷺ friends, Abu Bakr and Omar, were buried beside the Prophet when they died. Later, Muslims wanted to make the *masjid* bigger, so they expanded the *masjid* over the graves. Many other *sahabah* and good Muslims are buried in a place near the *masjid* called **Al-Baqea'**.

We love Prophet Muhammad ﷺ and his *sahabah*. That is why it is very special to visit his *masjid*, and the place where he is buried with his two best companions.

Al-Baqea'

The *masjid* is much bigger today than it was when Prophet Muhammad ﷺ was alive.

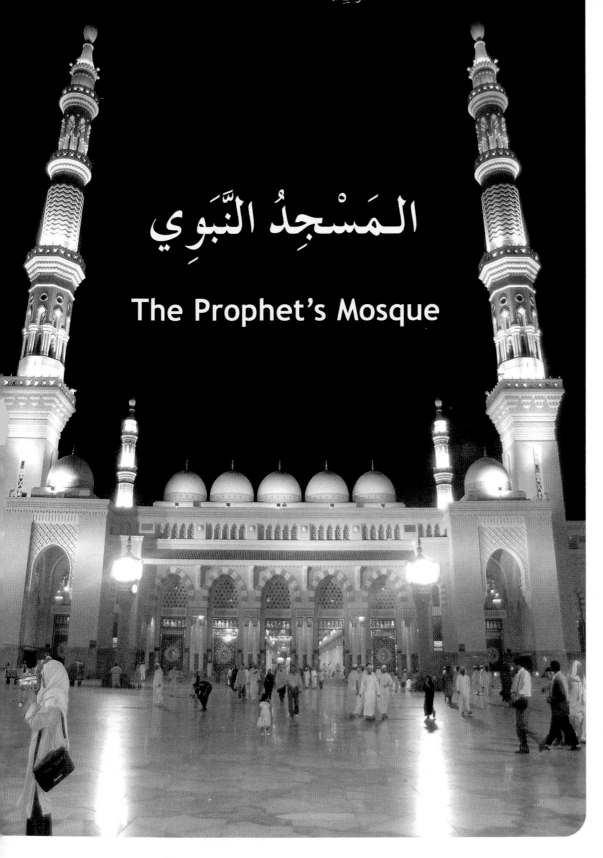

الْمَسْجِدُ النَّبَوِي

The Prophet's Mosque

The Prophet's ﷺ city is also called *Al-Madinah Al-Munawwarah*. This means, "The City of Light."

الْمَدِينَةُ الْمُنَوَّرة

The City of Light

ACTIVITY time

Draw *Al-Masjid-un-Nabawi* and hang your art in your room.

study

questions

1 Where is *Madinah*?

2 Why did early Muslims move there?

3 What special *masjid* is in *Madinah*?

4 Why is it special?

5 What was another name for *Madinah*?

UNIT D
CHAPTER 6

Al-Quds, Holy Jerusalem

questions?

1. Where is *Al-Quds*?
2. What *masjid* is in Jerusalem?
3. Who visits Jerusalem?

word watch

Bayt-ul-Maqdis	بَيْتُ المَقْدِسْ
Al-Quds	القُدسْ
Al-Masjid Al-Aqsa	المَسْجِدُ الأقْصى
Qubbat-us-Sakhrah	قُبَّة الصَّخْرَة
Al-Isra' Wal-Mi'raj	الإسْراء والمِعْراجْ
As-Sakhrah Al-Musharrafah	الصخرة المشرفة

PALESTINE BEFORE 1948

Al-Quds, or Jerusalem, is the third most special city for Muslims. It is in Palestine.

It was known as
"*Bayt-ul-Maqdis*."

This means "The Holy House."

بيت المقدس

There is a special *masjid* in Jerusalem. It is Al-*Masjid*-ul-Aqsa.

Al-*Masjid*-ul-Aqsa in *Al-Quds* (Jerusalem)

One special night, Prophet Muhammad ﷺ visited Al-*Masjid-ul-Aqsa* in *Al-Quds*. On that night, he prayed in the *masjid* with all the other prophets. He then stood on a special rock called **As-Sakhrah Al-Musharrafah** الصخرة المشرفة . From there, he went up to the heavens. That night is called *Al-Isra' Wal-Mi'raj* الإسراء والمعراج . Allah gave Prophet Muhammad ﷺ a very fast mount called Al-Buraq.

The place where Prophet Muhammad ﷺ left from Earth is covered by **Qubbat-us-Sakhrah** قبة الصخرة , the Dome of the Rock.

The Rock

Qubbat-us-Sakhrah, the Dome of the Rock.

WORDS OF WISDOM
Holy Qur'an

سورة الإسراء

Surah Al-Isra 17: 1

﴿ سُبْحَٰنَ ٱلَّذِىٓ أَسْرَىٰ بِعَبْدِهِۦ لَيْلًا مِّنَ ٱلْمَسْجِدِ ٱلْحَرَامِ إِلَى ٱلْمَسْجِدِ ٱلْأَقْصَا ٱلَّذِى بَٰرَكْنَا حَوْلَهُۥ لِنُرِيَهُۥ مِنْ ءَايَٰتِنَآ إِنَّهُۥ هُوَ ٱلسَّمِيعُ ٱلْبَصِيرُ ۝ ﴾

TRANSLITERATION

Subhan-allathee asra bi'abdihi laylam-mina almasjid-il-harami ila-almasjid-il-aqsa-allathee barakna hawlahu linuriyahu min ayatina innahu huwa-assamee'-ul-baseer.

TRANSLATION

Glorious is He Who made his servant travel by night from Al-Masjid-ul-Haram to Al-Masjid-ul-Aqsa whose environs We have blessed, so that We let him see some of Our signs. Surely, He is the All-Hearing, the All- Seeing. (1)

Jerusalem is different from *Makkah* and Al-*Madinah* because it is special to Muslims, Christians, and Jews.

This makes Jerusalem a special place for many people!

ACTIVITY time

Draw a picture of Al-*Masjid*-ul-Aqsa, and another of *Qubbat-us-Sakrah*, and hang them in your room.

study

questions

1 What is the third most special city for Muslims?

2 Who else is it special to?

3 What are some other names for Jerusalem?

4 What are some special buildings in Jerusalem?

5 What is special about the Dome of the Rock?

MY MUSLIM MANNERS

Allah Loves Kindness

questions?

1. Whom should we treat kindly?
2. How can good deeds help us?
3. How should we treat animals and plants?
4. What would happen if we were mean to people, animals, and plants?

word watch

[*Al-Lateef* اللَّطيفْ]

Did you know that even a small good deed can help you enter *Jannah*?

Also, a small bad deed can make Allah ﷻ displeased with you!

Allah loves us very much, and He wants us to love each other.

Allah is kind, and He wants us to be kind to each other.

We should be kind to our parents. We should obey and respect them all the time.

We should be kind to relatives, friends, and neighbors. We should respect them and help them whenever they need help.

We should even be kind to animals and plants. We should not hurt animals, or destroy flowers and good plants.

There are many kinds of animals in the world. Allah ﷻ created them all. We use some animals for food, like chicken.

Some animals are for riding, like horses. Some animals make good pets, like cats. They can be fun to play with!

Allah **is** Al-Lateef

اللطيف

The Kind

WORDS OF WISDOM

Hadeeth Shareef

حديث شريف

Narrated by Muslim.

عن شداد بن أوس رضي الله عنه: قال رسول الله ﷺ :
"إن الله كتب الإحسان على كل شيء"

TRANSLITERATION

"Inna-Allaha katab-al-Ihsana ala kulli Shay'."

TRANSLATION

Shaddad Ibn Aws reported that the Prophet ﷺ said: "Allah ordered that we be gentle with everything."

Allah ﷻ wants us to be kind to His creations.

Let us read a story that Prophet Muhammad ﷺ told us:

THE MAN AND THE DOG

Prophet Muhammad ﷺ said: Once a man was walking down the road. The man got very thirsty and he came to a well. He went to the well and had a long drink. When he was leaving, he saw a dog who was tired and thirsty. The man remembered how thirsty he felt before he drank, and he knew that the dog must have felt the same way.

The man went down into the well, filled his shoe with water, and helped the dog drink. Allah forgave all of the man's sins, gave him many *hasanat* and rewards, and promised him *Jannah*.

THE WOMAN AND THE CAT

Prophet Muhammad ﷺ told us another story about a woman who trapped a cat.

The woman did not give the cat food to eat. She did not let the cat go out to look for food.

The woman kept the cat inside until it died. Allah ﷻ was very angry with the woman, and He promised she would go to Hellfire.

WORDS OF WISDOM
(Hadeeth Shareef)

حديث شريف

Narrated By Bukhari

عن عائشة رضي الله عنها: قال رسول الله ﷺ :
"إِنَّ اللّهَ رَفِيقٌ يُحِبُّ الرِّفْقَ في الأَمْرِ كُلِّهِ"

TRANSLITERATION

"Inna-Allaha Rafeequn yuhibb-ur-rifqa fil-amri kullih."

TRANSLATION

Ai'sha رضي الله عنها reported that the Prophet ﷺ said:
"Allah is gentle. He loves kindness in every matter."

I want to be like the man who helped the dog and had all his bad deeds erased!

Me too! We should always be kind to people, animals, and plants, so we can go to *Jannah*, too! Muslims should always be kind!

healthy
habit

Be kind to people, animals, plants, and other things. Do not harm them. Take care of them.

study

questions

1. How does Allah want us to act with our parents, friends, plants and animals?

2. What is a name of Allah that means He is Kind?

3. What is a good way to treat an animal?

4. What is a bad way to treat an animal?

5. Should we step on or hurt flowers and good plants?

Ithaar and Caring

questions

1 Have you ever given away something you like to somebody else?
2 What can you do to show kindness to others?
3 How will we be rewarded if we care about each other?

word watch

[*Al-Kawthar* الكوثر
ithaar إيثار]

Helping the Poor

One day, Zaid and his classmates wanted to help their poor brothers and sisters around the world. They began collecting money in cans. Teacher Hibah told each student to call his or her can "My *Kawthar* Can."

Bilal asked Teacher Hibah: What is *Al-Kawthar*?

Teacher Hibah answered: It is a special river in Paradise (*Jannah*) that was given to our beloved Prophet Muhammad ﷺ by Allah ﷻ.

Mona: Why is the River of *Al-Kawthar* so special?

The River of Al-Kawthar is special for two reasons:

1 The Prophet ﷺ himself will give you a drink from this river on the Day of Judgment!

2 Its water is whiter than milk, and sweeter than honey!

The students collected the coins. They hoped Allah would let them drink from *Al-Kawthar* because they were sharing their money. Zaid took money from his allowance and put it in the cans.

We call this Ithaar.

Ithaar is when you give away something you love to someone else who needs it.

When you practice *ithaar*, you please Allah ﷻ, and your heart feels happy.

WORDS OF WISDOM

Holy Qur'an

سورة الكوثر

Surah Al-Kauther 108: 1-3

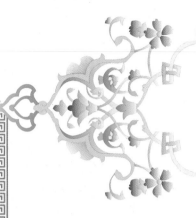

إِنَّآ أَعْطَيْنَكَ ٱلْكَوْثَرَ ﴿١﴾ فَصَلِّ لِرَبِّكَ وَٱنْحَرْ ﴿٢﴾ إِنَّ شَانِئَكَ هُوَ ٱلْأَبْتَرُ ﴿٣﴾

TRANSLITERATION

(1) Inna a'taynak-*Al-Kawthar*
(2) Fasalli lirabbika wanhar
(3) Inna shani'aka huwa-al-abtar

TRANSLATION

(O Prophet,) surely We have given to you Al-Kauthar. (1)
So, offer Salah (prayer) to your Lord, and sacrifice. (2)
Surely it is your enemy whose traces are cut off. (3)

AL-KAWTHAR الكوثر   AL-KAWTHAR الكوثر

Zaid and his friends collected the money with love and care. In one month, the students collected about 95 cans full of coins!

Teacher Hibah was very happy, and proud that her students were so kind and caring.

Leena Gives up Her Bed

Leena's aunt, uncle, and three cousins were coming from another country to visit for the summer. Leena was very excited. She helped her parents prepare the house for the visit. She helped set up mattresses for her cousins, but she knew her bed would be more comfortable to sleep on. She told her parents that she wanted to give up her bed for her cousins.

Mama: Why, Leena?

Leena: I want to practice *Ithaar*, and I want Allah ﷻ to reward me!

Mama was very proud of Leena.

WORDS OF WISDOM

Hadeeth Shareef

حديث شريف

Narrated By Muslim, Bukhari & Ahmad

عن أنس رضي الله عنه أن رسول الله ﷺ قال:
"لا يُؤْمِنُ أَحَدكم حتى يحب لأخيه ما يحب لنفسه."

TRANSLITERATION

"La yo'minu Ahadakum hatta yuhibba li akheehi ma yuhibbu linafsih."

TRANSLATION

Anas reported that the Prophet ﷺ said:
"You will not truly believe until one wishes for his brother or his neighbor what he wishes for himself."

healthy

habit

Always care about others, especially the needy. Try to practice *ithaar* all the time.

ACTIVITY time

You and your classmates can start your own "Can of *Kawthar*" using clean cans. Try to collect a good amount of money, and give it to the poor and the orphans.

study

questions

1 What does *ithaar* mean?

2 If you are selfish, would you be practicing *ithaar*?

3 Why is *Al-Kawthar* special?

4 Why did Leena give up her bed for her cousins?

5 Write down three ways you can show that you care for others.

I Obey My Parents

questions?

1. Who takes care of you at home?
2. Do you obey and care for him/her/them?
3. Why should you listen to your parents?
4. Who knows more, you or your parents?
5. Who knows even more than your parents?

word watch

[*birrul walidayn* بِرُّ الوالدين]

Mama watched Bilal run by.

Mama: Bilal, did you wash your hands?

Bilal: No, Mama, not yet.

Mama: You know you should wash your hands when you come home, dear. Remember to put your back-pack in your room.

healthy habit

Always keep yourself clean, and put your things in place. This makes Allah and your parents happy.

Bilal really wanted to go outside and play basketball, but he knew it was more important to listen to Mama.

He wanted to show that he loved her.

Bilal: Okay, Mama!
He picked up his backpack and took it to his room, and then he washed his hands.

Later on in the evening, Bilal was helping Mama in the kitchen with Sarah. He was so hungry! He opened a cabinet and took out some cookies.
He was just about to take a bite, and Sarah saw him.

Sarah: Bilal, it's almost dinner time. Baba says we shouldn't eat sweets right before dinner!

But Bilal was so hungry!

Bilal: Sarah, I'll just eat one cookie. Please?

Mama: Bilal, if you eat a cookie now, then you won't be able to finish your dinner! Besides, dinner is better for you than a cookie. That's why Baba says to wait for dessert.

At the dinner table, Mama smiled at Bilal.

Mama: Bilal has been a very good boy today. He listened to me and obeyed Baba even when he wanted to do something else.

Bilal: Because I know you tell me what is good for me!

Baba: This is *birrul walidayn*, that the Prophet ﷺ taught us.

Bilal: What is *birrul walidayn*, Dad?

Baba: It means obeying your parents and being kind to them. I used to obey my parents when I was young, and I still do. Allah ordered us to do so.

Mama: Also, when you obey your parents, you will make fewer mistakes, and all of us will be safe and happy.

Bilal and Sarah: We will always obey and respect you, Dad and Mom.

Our parents know more than we do.
We should listen to them.

Mama and Dad love us so much, Sarah! They tell us good things!

When we listen to our parents, we make Allah ﷻ happy.

healthy
habit

Always obey your parents, and do what they ask you to do before anything else. This makes Allah and your parents happy. The whole family will be happy too.

سورة الإسراء

Surhah Al-Isra 17: 23

وَقَضَىٰ رَبُّكَ أَلَّا تَعْبُدُوٓا۟ إِلَّآ إِيَّاهُ وَبِٱلْوَٰلِدَيْنِ إِحْسَٰنًا ۚ إِمَّا يَبْلُغَنَّ عِندَكَ ٱلْكِبَرَ أَحَدُهُمَآ أَوْ كِلَاهُمَا فَلَا تَقُل لَّهُمَآ أُفٍّ وَلَا تَنْهَرْهُمَا وَقُل لَّهُمَا قَوْلًا كَرِيمًا ﴿٢٣﴾

TRANSLITERATION

"Waqada rabbuka alla ta'budoo illa iyyahu wabilwali-dayni i hsana, imma yablughanna 'indak-al-kibara ahaduhuma aw kilahuma fala taqul lahuma offiw-wala tanharhuma waqul lahuma qawlan kareema."

TRANSLATION

Your Lord has decreed that you worship none but Him, and do good to parents. If any one of them or both of them reach old age, do not say to them: uff (a word or expression of anger or contempt) and do not scold them, and address them with respectful words, (23)

حديث شريف

Narrated By Abu Dawood

عن معاوية بن حيدة: قال يا رسول الله من أبر، قال: أمك ثم أمك ثم أمك ثم
أباك ثم الأقرب فالأقرب″

رواه أبو داود

TRANSLITERATION

"Mu'awiyah: Man Abarr? The Prophet: Ummak, thumma ummak, thumma ummak, thumma abak, thumm-al-aqrab fal-aqrab."

TRANSLATION

Mu'awiyah Ibn Haydah asked the Prophet ﷺ : Whom should I treat best? He said: "Your mother, your mother, your mother, and your father. Then your relatives."

study

questions

1 How did Bilal obey and listen to his parents?

2 Why did Mama ask Bilal to clean up before playing basketball?

3 Why did Baba say to wait until after dinner to eat sweets?

4 Whom do we make happy if we are good children?

5 Who will be kind to you if you are kind to your parents? What should you do if you disobey your parents?

I Am a Muslim; I Must Be Clean

questions?

1. Why must Muslims be clean?
2. What different things do you keep clean?
3. How do you help clean at home?

word watch

taharah	طهارة
najasah	نـجاسة
Al-Jumu'ah	الجُمعة

Taharah is purity and cleanliness.

Najasah means dirtiness, or impurity.

They are opposites. A Muslim should always practice *taharah*.

حديث شريف

Narrated By Muslim

عن أبي مالك الأشعري رضي الله عنه: قال رَسولُ اللَّه ﷺ :
"الطَّهور شَطْر الإيمانْ."

TRANSLITERATION

"At-Tahooru Shatr-ul-Iman"

TRANSLATION

Abu Malik reported that the Prophet ﷺ said:
"Purity is half of faith."

I keep myself clean

I love to take showers so that I smell nice and stay healthy.

We should especially take showers on Fridays because *Al-Jumu'ah* is a special day for Muslims.

I always wear clean clothes so that I look nice and neat.

Allah 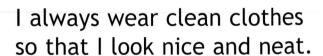 said:

"وثيابك فطَهِّر."

"Wa-thiyabaka fatahhir."
It means: "And purify your clothes." (74:4)

When I go to the bathroom I wash myself and my hands. I make sure to keep my clothes clean from *Najasah*. I keep the bathroom clean, too!

I brush my teeth and comb my hair.

Allah loves for our mouths to smell fresh when we pray. The Prophet 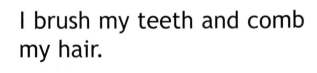 used a siwak to keep his teeth clean all the time.

I keep my house clean

I clean up after myself and put my things in place.

I keep my masjid clean

I keep my school clean

I keep my Earth clean

study

questions

1 What does *taharah* mean? What is the opposite?

2 What are some things you do to make yourself clean?

3 How do you help keep your home clean?

4 What are other places you can think of to keep clean?

5 What did the Prophet ﷺ say about purity or cleanliness?

A Dinner in Our Neighbor's Home

questions?

1. Do you ever go to your friend's house for dinner?
2. What do you do there?
3. How can you be a good guest?

word watch

Yameen   يَمين
Shimal   شِمال

"Leena and Zaid, we are going to Bilal's house for dinner on Friday InshaAllah," said their mother. Leena and Zaid jumped up and down because they were very excited!

They were smiling from ear to ear!

Bilal and Sarah were very excited too! At school, Bilal told Zaid about the games they were going to play together.

Bilal said: "First we'll eat dinner, and then we can play all night long. We'll have a blast!"

He had the plan all figured out.

"We can play Race to *Al-Ka'bah*!" Leena and Sarah said at the same time. They just had to wait until tomorrow.

Friday finally came! Zaid's father woke him up for *Fajr*, and he jumped out of bed!

Zaid and Leena went to school. At home, even baby Yusuf was excited!

After school, Leena and Zaid started getting ready for dinner. Then they heard their father's voice, "Are we ready to go?"

Zaid and Leena ran downstairs. When everyone sat down in the car, Leena started to recite the traveling du'aa, and the whole family joined in.

healthy
habits

When you leave home say:

"بسم الله، توكلنا على الله، لا حول ولا قوة إلا بالله."

" *Bismillah*, tawakkalna alAllah, la hawla wala quwwata illa billah"

It means: In the name of Allah, we rely on Allah. We have no power without Allah.

When you enter the house say:

"بسم الله ولجنا، وبسم الله خرجنا، اللهم إنا نسألك خير المولج وخير المخرج."

"Bismillahi walajna, wa-bismillahi kharajna, allahuma inna nas'alula khayr-al-mawloj wa khayr-al-makhraj"

It means: With the name of Allah we enter, and with the name of Allah we exit. O Allah we ask of You a good entering and a good exit.

★★★★★★★★★★★★★★★★★★★★★★★★

Learn to say this du'aa when you are leaving to go somewhere:

"سُبحان الذي سخر لنا هذا وما كنا له مُقْرِنِين وإنَّا إلى ربنا لمنقلبون."

"Subhan-Allathi Sakhara lana hatha wa ma kunna lahu muqrineen wa inna ila rabbina lamunqaliboon."

It means: Glory be to Allah who made this (car) available to us. And we will not worship others with Him. We are all returning to Allah in the Hereafter.

Finally, they reached Bilal's house! Zaid ran to ring the doorbell. Bilal answered the door.

"*Assalamu Alaykum*!" Bilal said.
"Wa alaykum assalaam!" said Zaid's Family.
The children all said, "Let's go play!"

Bilal's parents welcomed Zaid's family.
Everyone was smiling!

After a while, dinner was ready.
Bilal's Mom said: "Okay kids, go wash up before we eat dinner."
All the children went to wash their hands and mouths.

Everyone sat down at the table. Zaid was so hungry! Bilal's mother asked if everyone said their du'aa to thank Allah before they ate.

healthy
h a b i t

Always say this du'aa before you eat:

"اللهم بارك لنا في ما رزقتنا وقنا عذاب النّار، بسم الله ."

"Allahumma barik lana feema razaqtana wa-qina athab-an-nar, *bismillah*."

This means: "O Allah! Bless (the food) You gave us and save us from the punishment of the Hellfire. In the name of Allah."

WORDS OF WISDOM
Hadeeth Shareef

حديث شريف

Narrated by Al-Bukhari and Muslim

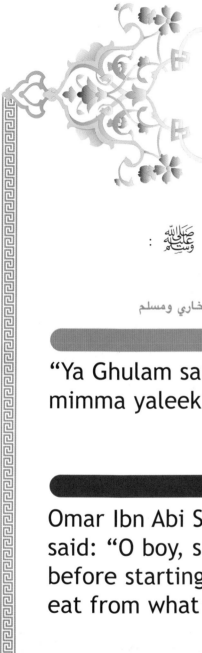

عن عمر بن أبي سلمة رضي الله عنه: قال لي رسول الله ﷺ: "يا غلام، سمِّ الله وكل بيمينك وكل مما يليك."

رواه البخاري ومسلم

TRANSLITERATION

"Ya Ghulam sammillah, wa-kul biyameenik, wa kul mimma yaleek."

TRANSLATION

Omar Ibn Abi Salamah reported that the Prophet ﷺ said: "O boy, say Allah's name, (i.e., say *Bismillah* before starting eating), eat with your right hand, and eat from what is near you."

E33

Zaid began to get silly. He took some of his mashed potatoes and put them on Bilal's nose! They were giggling! Bilal tried to do it back to Zaid, and he accidentally spilled his father's drink!

The boys weren't laughing anymore. Zaid's mother asked them to stop playing with their food. The boys cleaned up the mess, and they promised not to make this mistake again.

Leena wanted to drink all of her juice at once. She was drinking with her left hand. Her father kindly told her, "The Prophet ﷺ taught us to drink one sip at a time, and not to finish our cup in less than three sips." Also, He taught us to eat and drink with our *yameen* (right hand) not our *shimal* (our left hand).

Zaid, Sarah, Bilal, and Leena's parents were very happy that the children did not waste their food.

After they finished eating, the families began to say the du'aa of finishing a meal. This time, Zaid's father told everyone what it meant.

Zaid and Leena smiled at Bilal's mother and said, "Jazakum Allah Khayran for your yummy food!"

It was a nice thing to say!

healthy
habit

Say this du'aa after you finish eating:

"الحمد للّه الذي أطعمنا وسقانا وجعلنا مسلمين."

*"Alhamdulillah al-lathi at'amana
wa saqana wa ja'alana Muslimeen."*

This means, "All praise is due to Allah ﷻ Who gave us food and drink and made us Muslims."

Bilal's mother replied: "Wa iyyakum, Leena and Zaid. We are all glad you came!"

When everyone was getting up, Leena, Zaid, and Bilal noticed that the mothers were clearing the table. They wanted to help, too! It would show their mothers that they were thankful for the dinner.

After dinner the children played some more, but then it was time to go.

Zaid's dad called the children.

"It's time to go; let's get our shoes on."

Zaid and Leena did not want to leave, but they knew it was important to listen to their parents.

Bilal's family thanked their guests for coming. "Jazakum Allah khayran for having us!" Leena and Zaid said.

"Wa iyyakum!" Bilal's parents said.
Everyone said "*Assalamu Alaykum*" and said good-bye to a fun night!

healthy habit

Always be very polite when you are at other people's houses.

study questions

1. What should you say when you meet a Muslim brother or sister?

2. What should you do and say before and after you eat?

3. Which hand should you eat with? Why?

4. Is it a good idea to play with your food? What can happen if you play with your food?

5. How can you show that you are thankful to your parents?

Leena and Zaid Sleep over at Their Grandparents' House

questions?

1. What should we do when an elder tells us to do something?
2. What are some things you need to do before going to bed?
3. What is the best way to sleep?
4. What is the first thing you should do in the morning?

word watch

[*Al-Mu'awwithat* المُعَوِّذاتْ]

Leena and Zaid loved visiting their grandparents. They used to wait for the holidays to come so Mama and Dad would take them over to their grandparents' house. Leena and Zaid slept over there on vacations. They were always excited to be with their grandparents.

On *Eid* day, everyone visited their grandparents' house. They enjoyed eating dinner together and sharing stories. When Leena and Zaid's parents left, they stayed to spend the night.

When bedtime came, Leena and Zaid did not want to go to sleep. They wanted to hear more stories from their grandparents. Leena and Zaid's grandmother said, "We will finish our stories in the morning. Now, it is time to go to bed." Leena and Zaid obeyed their grandmother right away.

They brushed their teeth.

They put on their pajamas.

They hugged and said good-night to their grandparents.

Leena and Zaid's grandmother tucked them into bed and reminded them to say their du'aa.

Their grandmother also reminded them of Ayat Al-Kursi and *Al-Mu'awwithat*, which are *Surat al-Falaq* and *Surat An-Nas*. The du'aa and *Al-Qur'an* are protection for us from Shaytan.

Leena, Zaid, and their grandmother said the du'aa and the suwar all together. Leena and Zaid kissed their grandmother goodnight and gave her a big hug.

When grandmother was leaving the room, she noticed Leena and Zaid were about to sleep on their stomachs. She told them how Prophet Muhammad ﷺ taught us that it is better to sleep on our right side or our back. Leena and Zaid thanked their grandmother for teaching them that.

healthy
h a b i t

1. Memorize this du'aa and say it every night before you go to sleep.

"بِاسْمِكَ اللّٰهُمَّ أَمُوتُ وَأَحْيا."

"Bissmika Allahumma Amoutu Wa Ahya."

It means:"By Your Name, O Allah, I die and live."

2. Read Ayat Al-Kursiand *Al-Mu'awwithat* before you sleep too.

ACTIVITY time

Make a checklist that you can use before you go to bed. Here's an idea of how it can look:

BEDTIME TASK   **DONE?**

1. Say "*Assalamu Alaykum*, **goodnight**" to your parents ○
2. Change your clothes ○
3. Brush your teeth ○
4. Make *Wudoo'* ○
5. Pray 'Isha ○
6. Say your du'aa and Mu'awwithat ○
7. Sleep on your right side ○

Allah ﷻ made the night so we can rest our bodies and minds. Allah said in the Qur'an,

"وجعلنا نومكم سُباتا"

"And We made your sleep for rest."

An-Naba' 9

Sleeping is a gift from Allah.

Allah ﷻ made the day so we can work and learn. Allah said in the Qur'an:

"وجعلنا النهار معاشا"

"And We made the day for livelihood."

An-Naba' 11

When you wake up in the morning, you should thank Allah ﷻ for giving you another day.

At *Fajr*, Leena and Zaid's grandparents woke them up to pray. They were very proud of them for doing a great job in *salah*.

After breakfast, Leena and Zaid's grandparents finished their stories as they had promised. Soon, Mama and Dad came to pick them up. Leena and Zaid thanked their grandparents with a hug and a kiss for taking such good care of them, and they all said, "*Assalamu Alaykum!*"

healthy
habit

Be a morning person. Sleep early to wake up early. Start your day early at *Fajr* time and sleep right after *Isha'* time.

healthy
habit

When you wake up in the morning, say:

"الحمد لله الذي أحيانا بعد ما أماتنا وإليه النشور."

"Al-Hamdu lillah-il-lathi ahyana ba'da ma amatana wa-ilayh-in-nushoor."

It means: "Praise be to Allah for giving us life after death, and to Him we will return."

WORDS OF WISDOM
Holy Qur'an

المعوذات

Al-Mu'awwithat

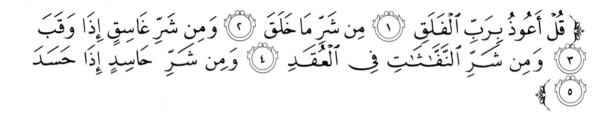

قُلْ أَعُوذُ بِرَبِّ الْفَلَقِ ۞ مِن شَرِّ مَا خَلَقَ ۞ وَمِن شَرِّ غَاسِقٍ إِذَا وَقَبَ ۞ وَمِن شَرِّ النَّفَّاثَاتِ فِي الْعُقَدِ ۞ وَمِن شَرِّ حَاسِدٍ إِذَا حَسَدَ ۞

قُلْ أَعُوذُ بِرَبِّ النَّاسِ ۞ مَلِكِ النَّاسِ ۞ إِلَـٰهِ النَّاسِ ۞ مِن شَرِّ الْوَسْوَاسِ الْخَنَّاسِ ۞ الَّذِي يُوَسْوِسُ فِي صُدُورِ النَّاسِ ۞ مِنَ الْجِنَّةِ وَالنَّاسِ ۞

TRANSLITERATION

(1) Qul a'oothu birabb-il-falaq
(2) Min sharri ma khalaq
(3) Wamin sharri ghasiqin itha waqab
(4) Wamin sharr-in-naffathati fil-'uqad
(5) Wamin sharri hasidin itha hasad

(1) Qul a'oothu birabb-in-nas
(2) Malik-in-nas
(3) Ilah-in-nas
(4) Min sharr-il-waswas-il-khannasi
(5) Allathee yuwaswisu fee sudoor-in-nas
(6) Min aljinnati wannas

TRANSLATION

Surah Al-Falaq 113: 1-5

Say, "I seek refuge with the Lord of the daybreak (1) From the evil of everything He has created, (2) And from the evil of the dark night when it penetrates, (3) And from the evil of the women who blow on the knots, (4) And from the evil of an envier when he envies. (5)

Surah An-Nas 114: 1-6

Say, "I seek refuge with the Lord of mankind, (1) The King of mankind, (2) The God of mankind, (3) From the evil of the whisperer who withdraws (when Allah's name is pronounced), (4) The one who whispers in the hearts of people, (5) Whether from among the Jinn or Mankind. (6)

Listen to these surahs on Track 20 of your CD.

study

questions

1 Did Leena and Zaid obey their grandmother when she said it was time for bed? What do you learn from that?

2 What du'aa and suwar did their grandmother remind them to say before they slept?

3 Is it good to sleep on your stomach? What is the best way to sleep?

4 Why did Allah create night? Why did He create day?

5 What is the first thing you should say when you wake up?

I Love Islam
Level 1

INDEX

INDEX